$\mathcal{Y}$ou won't b

THE LOW-FAT, 150-CALORIE DESSERT COOKBOOK
is filled with delicious recipes for health-minded dessert lovers.

Brownies, custards, cakes, pastries . . .
Fruit tarts, cheesecake, cookies, pie . . .

You'll find all your favorite desserts without excess fat
and calories—so you can enjoy desserts and
feel great about it!

The
Low-Fat,
150-Calorie
Dessert Cookbook

Nancy S. Hughes is the author of other such healthful
cookbooks as: *The Four-Course 400-Calorie Meal Cookbook*
and *The 300-Calorie One-Dish Meal Cookbook*.

The Low-Fat, 150-Calorie Dessert Cookbook

NANCY S. HUGHES

BERKLEY BOOKS *New York*

Note: Although brand names are referred to in the following recipes, they are used for illustrative purposes and similar brands may suffice.

THE LOW-FAT, 150-CALORIE DESSERT COOKBOOK

A Berkley Book / published by arrangement with
the author

PRINTING HISTORY
Berkley trade paperback edition / October 1994

ISBN: 0-425-15827-6

BERKLEY®
Berkley Books are published by The Berkley Publishing Group,
200 Madison Avenue, New York, New York 10016.
Berkley and the "B" design
are trademarks belonging to Berkley Publishing Corporation.

PRINTED IN THE UNITED STATES OF AMERICA

10 9 8 7 6 5 4 3 2 1

Dedication

To my mother—whom I love for what she was, for what she always will be to me . . . my best friend.

Contents

Apple Turnovers • Freshly Baked Cinnamon Rolls • Frozen Chocolate Eclairs • Frozen Kahlua Meringue

Those Succulent Fruits   111

Preface

I love having ice cream sandwiches on the front porch steps with my little ones.

I love sitting down close to the fire with warm bread pudding on a cold winter's night.

I love sharing cookies and milk when my children come home from school chatting about their day.

I love curling up with a good book in the quiet of the night with a piece of chocolate cake.

I love waking up to the smell of homemade muffins in the oven.

I love relaxing on the patio after dinner on a warm summer's night with my husband and a piece of fresh strawberry pie.

I love making the dessert a grand affair when entertaining my special friends.

I love desserts and I'll never give them up. Desserts and good times go hand in hand. Don't live without the sweet things in life anymore.

Enjoy!

Acknowledgments

Special thanks to my children, Will, Annie, and Taft, and my husband, Greg, for your honesty, directness, and, above all, your sense of humor. You are, by far, my most respected critics.

And, to my father, for showing me how to pursue my chosen goals and have a good time getting there.

Introduction

Real desserts, the truly scrumptious ones, don't have to be that taboo treat at the end of the meal anymore.

In my book, I've created rich and hearty *real* desserts, not airy excuses—all low in fat and never more than 150 calories per serving.

We work all day with stresses and deadlines and at the end of the day, we want and need comfort and relief. To many people, desserts offer just that, but at the same time, eating calorie- and fat-laden desserts causes more stress if the momentary pleasure is followed by the dreaded guilt. Now it's time to stop, relax, and enjoy that dessert for all its worth.

The recipes range from cookies for kids of all ages to the chocolate lover's dream. All are easy to prepare and come in normal to large-size portions—no skimpy servings allowed.

The calories and fat content have been measured according to Bowes and Church's *Food Values of Portions Commonly Used,* which is a recognized reference used by hospitals in order to ensure that the fat and calorie content is consistently and reliably low.

This book was written not only to eliminate that splurge-and-guilt syndrome, but to eliminate those feelings of being deprived of special comforts and to enjoy desserts the way they were intended to be enjoyed—pleasurably and without an ounce of guilt.

Cakes—The Forbidden Wonders

Rich and Warm Brownie Decadence with Raspberry Sauce

Very chocolate, very moist brownie-type wedges dusted in a lace pattern with powdered sugar and served with a bit of light raspberry sauce

1½ cups plus 1 tablespoon all-purpose flour

¼ cup cocoa powder

1½ teaspoons baking powder

¼ teaspoon baking soda

½ cup plus 1 tablespoon granulated sugar

2 tablespoons plus 2 teaspoons vegetable oil

¼ cup egg substitute

2 teaspoons vanilla extract

1 tablespoon water

1 8-inch paper doily

1 tablespoon powdered sugar

¼ cup low-sugar raspberry spread

Preheat oven to 350 degrees.

Coat a 9-inch cake pan with low-calorie cooking spray and line with waxed paper.

In medium bowl, combine flour, cocoa powder, baking powder, and baking soda. Blend well.

Combine sugar, oil, egg substitute, vanilla, and water. Mix thoroughly.

Make a well in center of dry ingredients. Pour in wet ingredients. Using a rubber spatula, gently fold ingredients together until just blended. Batter will be thick and lumpy. Spoon into prepared baking pan. Spread to cover bottom of pan evenly.

Bake exactly 18 minutes. Do not cook longer. Remove from oven and place pan on wire rack. Cool slightly, 5 minutes.

Carefully invert onto decorative plate. Lay paper doily over brownie cake. Using sifter, sift powdered sugar over top of doily. Very carefully remove doily, leaving lace pattern. Discard doily and any remaining sugar.

Over low heat, melt raspberry spread. Serve each with 1½ teaspoons sauce spooned around outer edges of each slice.

Serve warm.

SERVES 8; 5.2 FAT GRAMS AND 31% CALORIES FROM FAT PER SERVING.

Easy Chocolate Sheet Cake with Mocha Frosting

A "quick and easy" for the chocolate lover

- 1 Duncan Hines Devil's Food packaged cake mix
- ½ cup egg substitute
- 1½ cups water
- 3 tablespoons cocoa powder
- 1 8-ounce container light whipped topping

Preheat oven to 325 degrees.

In medium mixing bowl, combine cake mix, egg substitute, and water. Using an electric mixer at low speed, scraping bottom and sides with rubber spatula, beat 3 minutes. Coat a 15-inch × 10-inch jelly roll pan with low-calorie cooking spray and pour batter in pan. Spread batter evenly in pan and bake 18 minutes or until wooden pick inserted comes out clean.

While cake is baking, gently but thoroughly fold cocoa powder into whipped topping. Refrigerate. When cake is done, place pan on wire rack. Cool cake completely in pan, about 2 hours.

When cake has completely cooled, top cake with frosting. Refrigerate until serving time.

SERVES 18; 4.2 FAT GRAMS AND 25% CALORIES FROM FAT PER SERVING.

LIGHT AMBROSIA CAKE

A "quick and easy" cleverly disguised

1 Duncan Hines Butter Recipe
   cake mix
1½ cups water
½ cup egg substitute
1 tablespoon grated orange rind
3 egg whites, room temperature

1 teaspoon vanilla extract
¼ teaspoon cream of tartar
¼ cup granulated sugar
2 fresh navel oranges, sectioned
   and diced
⅔ cup (1¾ ounces) canned
   sweetened coconut

Preheat oven to 325 degrees.

Coat a 15-inch × 10-inch jelly roll pan with low-calorie cooking spray.

In mixing bowl, combine cake mix, water, and egg substitute. Using an electric mixer on low speed, blend until just moistened. Add orange rind. Scraping sides and bottom with a rubber spatula, beat 2 additional minutes on medium speed. Pour batter into prepared pan and bake 18 minutes or until wooden pick inserted comes out clean. Place pan on wire rack and cool completely.

Using an electric mixer on high speed, beat egg whites until foamy. Add vanilla and cream of tartar, and beat until soft peaks form. Gradually add sugar, 1 tablespoon at a time, and beat until stiff peaks form. Do not overbeat.

When cake has cooled, arrange diced oranges on top of cake.

Spoon frosting on top and gently spread over cake, careful not to disturb oranges. Top with shredded coconut and refrigerate overnight, or at least 8 hours.

SERVES 20; 3.6 FAT GRAMS AND 22% CALORIES FROM FAT PER SERVING.

Variation: For larger servings, follow Basic Cake Roll recipe on page 17, adding the orange rind, and top with oranges, frosting, and coconut. Serves 12; 3.4 fat grams and 21% calories from fat per serving.

SWEET PINEAPPLE-ORANGE PUDDING CAKE

A "quick and easy" with the taste of homemade

- 1 Duncan Hines Butter Recipe cake mix
- ½ cup egg substitute
- 1½ cups water
- ½ 3-ounce package instant sugar-free vanilla pudding mix
- 1 cup skim milk

- 2 egg whites, room temperature
- 2 8-ounce cans crushed pineapple in its own juice, undrained
- 2 8-ounce cans mandarin oranges in light syrup, drained

Preheat oven to 325 degrees.

In medium mixing bowl, combine cake mix, egg substitute, and water. Using an electric mixer at medium speed and scraping bottom and sides with rubber spatula, beat 3 minutes. Coat a jelly roll pan with low-calorie cooking spray and pour batter in pan. Spread batter evenly in pan and bake 18 minutes or until wooden pick inserted comes out clean. Remove from oven and place pan on wire rack. Cool cake completely in pan.

Combine pudding mix and milk in bowl. Beat until smooth and let stand 5 minutes. Using clean, dry beaters, beat egg whites until stiff peaks form. Gently but thoroughly fold into pudding mixture. Spread evenly over cake.

Combine undrained pineapple with drained oranges. Mix well and spoon, by teaspoonfuls, over cake. Cover with plastic wrap and chill overnight or at least 8 hours.

SERVES 20; 2.5 FAT GRAMS AND 15% CALORIES FROM FAT PER SERVING.

Variation: *For large servings, follow Basic Cake Roll recipe on page 17; top with pudding mixture, pineapple, and oranges. Serves 12; 1.6 fat grams and 9% calories from fat per serving.*

FAT-FREE ANGEL FOOD CAKE

Cake without guilt

12 egg whites, room temperature
1½ teaspoons cream of tartar
2 teaspoons vanilla extract
½ teaspoon almond extract

1 cup granulated sugar, divided
¾ cup sifted cake flour
¼ teaspoon salt

Preheat oven to 350 degrees.

In a large mixing bowl, using an electric mixer on high speed, beat egg whites with cream of tartar, vanilla extract, and almond extract until soft peaks form. Gradually add ¼ cup of the sugar, 1 tablespoon at a time, and continue beating until stiff peaks form.

Combine flour, salt, and the remaining ¾ cup sugar. Sift ¼ cup of the flour mixture over whipped egg whites and gently fold together. Repeat process until all flour mixture is folded in. Pour batter into an ungreased 10-inch tube pan. Bake 45 minutes or until cake springs back when lightly touched. Invert pan and cool in pan on wire rack one hour. Run knife around edges of pan and remove. Return cake to wire rack and cool completely.

PLAIN CAKE SERVES 9; 0 FAT GRAMS AND 0% CALORIES FROM FAT.

Angel Food Cake with Fresh Peaches and Nectarines

Angel food cake piled high with fruits marinated in plum wine with a hint of ginger

- 1 Fat-Free Angel Food Cake recipe, page 9
- ¾ cup plum wine
- 1½ cups fresh peach slices
- 1½ cups fresh nectarine slices (2 medium)
- 1 cup sweet dark cherries, approximately 20, halved and pitted
- ¼ teaspoon ground ginger

Follow the basic angel food cake recipe. Cool completely and cover with plastic wrap.

In small saucepan, add wine, bring to boil, reduce heat, and simmer uncovered 3 minutes. Cool completely, pour over sliced fruit, add ginger, toss well, and refrigerate overnight or at least 4 hours.

At time of serving, slice cake and spoon ⅓ cup of fruit mixture over each slice.

SERVES 12; 0.2 FAT GRAM AND 1% CALORIES FROM FAT PER SERVING.

Angel Food Cake with Vanilla-Almond Sauce

Freshly baked and slightly warm angel food slices served with a golden almond sauce

1 Fat-Free Angel Food Cake
  recipe, page 9
1 cup water
2 teaspoons cornstarch
¼ cup dark brown sugar, packed

2 teaspoons almond extract
2 tablespoons diet margarine
⅓ cup almond slices, toasted

Follow the basic angel food cake recipe. While cake is cooling, in a small saucepan, combine water, cornstarch, and sugar. Bring to boil; stirring with a flat spatula, continue to boil 2 minutes. Remove from heat and stir in almond extract and margarine. Stir to blend thoroughly.

After removing cake from pan, while cake is still warm, carefully slice cake using a serrated knife. Sprinkle almonds over all and pour warm sauce evenly over all. Serve warm. (May need to reheat sauce over low heat before pouring over cake.)

SERVES 12; 2.6 FAT GRAMS AND 15% CALORIES FROM FAT PER SERVING.

Variation: For individual servings, use 1¼ teaspoons crumbled almonds plus 2 tablespoons sauce on 1/12 of cake.

Chocolate Affair

A rich chocolate sponge cake with raspberry filling smothered by light chocolate whipped topping and crowned with toasted almonds

¾ cup sifted cake flour
¾ cup granulated sugar, divided
⅓ cup plus 2 tablespoons unsweetened cocoa powder, divided
2 teaspoons baking powder
¼ teaspoon salt
½ cup plus 2 tablespoons strong brewed coffee, room temperature

1 teaspoon almond extract
10 egg whites, room temperature
2 cups light whipped topping
⅔ cup low-sugar raspberry spread
1 ounce (scant ¼ cup) sliced almonds, toasted and crumbled

Preheat oven to 350 degrees.

In a small bowl, sift together cake flour, ½ cup of the sugar, ⅓ cup of the cocoa powder, baking powder, and salt. Add coffee and almond extract. Stir to blend and set aside.

In a large bowl, beat egg whites until soft peaks form. Gradually add remaining ¼ cup sugar. Beat until stiff peaks form. Gently fold in reserved flour and coffee mixture. Pour batter into an ungreased 10-inch tube pan. Bake 40 minutes or until cake springs back when lightly touched.

While cake is baking, gently but thoroughly fold remaining 2 tablespoons cocoa powder into whipped topping. Chill until needed.

Remove cake from oven. Invert cake and place on rack. Cool cake 1 hour and then remove from pan. Using a serrated knife, cut cake crosswise to make 3 layers. Spread ⅓ cup raspberry spread on bottom layer. Place second layer on top of the spread. Spoon the remaining ⅓ cup of the spread on cake. Top with third layer and ice entire cake with the chilled topping. Refrigerate at least 8 hours. At time of serving, sprinkle the top with almonds.

SERVES 12; 3.2 FAT GRAMS AND 19% CALORIES FROM FAT PER SERVING.

LEMON YOGURT ANGEL FOOD CAKE WITH FRESH LEMON GLAZE

Light, lemony, mousse-filled cake with a pleasantly lemoned glaze

12 egg whites, room temperature
1½ teaspoons cream of tartar
½ teaspoon almond extract
2 teaspoons vanilla extract
1 cup granulated sugar, divided
¾ cup all-purpose flour
1 teaspoon lemon zest, divided

1 cup light lemon yogurt
1 cup light whipped topping
1 tablespoon plus 2 teaspoons lemon juice, divided
½ cup powdered sugar
2 teaspoons water

Preheat oven to 350 degrees.

In a large mixing bowl, using an electric mixer on high speed, beat egg whites with cream of tartar and the almond and vanilla extracts until soft peaks form. Gradually add ¼ cup of the sugar, 1 tablespoon at a time, and continue beating until stiff peaks form.

Combine flour, salt and the remaining ¾ cup of the sugar. Sift ¼ cup of the flour mixture over whipped egg white mixture and gently fold together. Repeat process until all flour mixture is folded in. Fold in ½ teaspoon of the lemon zest. Pour batter into an ungreased 10-inch tube pan. Bake 45 minutes or until cake springs back when lightly touched. Invert pan and cool in pan on wire rack one hour. Run knife around edges of pan and remove. Return cake to wire rack and cool completely.

In small bowl, gently fold lemon yogurt, whipped topping, and 2 teaspoons of the lemon juice together and refrigerate while cake is cooling.

Combine the remaining tablespoon lemon juice and ½ teaspoon lemon zest with powdered sugar and water. Stir until smooth.

When cake is cool, using a serrated knife, cut cake crosswise. Spoon lemon yogurt mixture on bottom layer, allowing mixture to run over sides occasionally. Top with second layer and drizzle glaze over all. Refrigerate overnight or at least 4 hours.

SERVES 12; 0.7 FAT GRAM AND 4% CALORIES FROM FAT PER SERVING.

Fresh Orange Angel Food Cake

A light angel food cake, drizzled with a lightly sweetened, lightly pungent orange sauce, crowned with whipped topping and fresh oranges

1 Fat-Free Angel Food Cake recipe, page 9
2 cups orange juice
2 tablespoons granulated sugar
1 tablespoon cornstarch
½ teaspoon grated orange rind
1 cup light whipped topping
1 large navel orange, sectioned and diced

Follow the basic angel food cake recipe. While cake is cooling, in a small saucepan, combine orange juice, sugar, and cornstarch. Blend thoroughly. Bring to boil, and boil until it thickens, about 1–2 minutes. Remove from heat and let stand 10 minutes; stir in orange rind.

When cake has cooled, pour sauce over top, allowing sauce to drizzle down sides. Refrigerate overnight, or at least 4 hours.

At time of serving, place 1 tablespoon whipped topping and 1 tablespoon fresh orange pieces on top of each slice.

SERVES 12; 0.8 FAT GRAM AND 5% CALORIES FROM FAT PER SERVING.

Variation: *At time of serving, crown the entire cake with whipped topping and top with fresh orange pieces. Slice and serve.*

Basic Cake Roll

A lightly sweetened sponge-type cake

3 egg yolks	½ cup cake flour
½ cup granulated sugar, divided	1 teaspoon baking powder
1 teaspoon vanilla extract	¼ teaspoon salt
5 egg whites, room temperature	2 tablespoons powdered sugar

Preheat oven to 350 degrees.

Coat the bottom and sides of a 15-inch × 10-inch × 1-inch jelly roll pan with low-calorie cooking spray. Line with waxed paper and set aside.

In a large bowl, using an electric mixer on high speed, beat egg yolks until thick and lemon-colored. Gradually add ¼ cup of the sugar, beating until sugar is dissolved. Stir in vanilla extract.

Clean and thoroughly dry beaters. In separate bowl, beat egg whites on high speed until soft peaks form. Gradually add the remaining ¼ cup sugar, 1 tablespoon at a time, and continue beating until stiff peaks form.

Add flour, baking powder, and salt to egg yolks.

Stir until just blended. Gently yet thoroughly fold in egg whites to egg yolk mixture and pour batter evenly into the prepared pan. Bake 12 minutes or until wooden pick comes out clean when inserted into cake.

To prepare for filling, immediately remove from pan onto a clean towel dusted with powdered sugar. Quickly but carefully remove waxed paper. Start at narrow end, roll cake and towel together; cool roll on wire rack 1 hour. Unroll and fill. Roll, placing seam side down.

SERVES 8; 116 CALORIES, 2.2 FAT GRAMS, AND 2% CALORIES FROM FAT PER SERVING.

Variation: For an easy, extra-large-serving dessert, simply cool cake in pan, cut to serve 8. Toss 4 cups sliced strawberries with 2 tablespoons granulated sugar. Let stand at least 15 minutes and spoon ½ cup berries over each serving.

SERVES 8; 150 CALORIES, 2.5 FAT GRAMS AND 2% CALORIES FROM FAT PER SERVING.

Apple and Raisin–Filled Cake Roll

A fresh apple and raisin filling in a lightly spiced cake roll

1 Basic Cake Roll recipe, page 17
½ cup plus 1 tablespoon light brown sugar,
1½ teaspoons apple pie spice, divided
½ cup apple juice
2 teaspoons cornstarch
2½ cups Golden Delicious apple slices, thinly cut

1 cup Granny Smith apple slices, thinly cut
¼ cup raisins
1 teaspoon lemon juice
1 teaspoon vanilla extract
1 tablespoon granulated sugar
½ teaspoon ground cinnamon

Follow the Basic Cake Roll recipe, using ½ cup light brown sugar instead of granulated sugar and adding 1 teaspoon of the apple pie spice to batter; omit powdered sugar. While cake is rolled and cooling, prepare filling.

In medium saucepan, combine apple juice and cornstarch and blend well. Add apple slices, raisins, lemon juice, 1 tablespoon brown sugar, and ½ teaspoon apple pie spice. Stir well. Bring to a boil, reduce heat, cover tightly, and simmer 3 minutes. Remove apple mixture from heat, stir in vanilla extract, and set aside to cool slightly, about 5 minutes. Unroll cake. Spread apple mixture evenly over cake roll. Gently roll, placing seam side down. Combine granulated sugar and cinnamon, blend well, and sprinkle over rolled cake.

SERVES 10; 2 FAT GRAMS AND 12% CALORIES FROM FAT PER SERVING.

$\mathscr{B}$ANANA PUDDING CAKE ROLL

A delicate cake roll filled with fresh bananas and vanilla mousse pudding with a hint of nutmeg

1 Basic Cake Roll recipe, page 17
2 large bananas, thinly sliced
1 small package instant sugar-free vanilla pudding mix

2 cups skim milk
2 egg whites, room temperature
Nutmeg

Preheat oven to 350 degrees.

Follow the Basic Cake Roll recipe, omitting powdered sugar and baking in two 8-inch round cake pans coated with cooking spray and lined with waxed paper. Bake 12–14 minutes. Remove from pans and place on wire rack to cool completely. Arrange banana slices on top.

In a medium bowl, add pudding mix and milk. Blend until smooth. Set aside.

In nonplastic bowl (which will better preserve egg-whites' volume), using an electric mixer on high speed, beat egg whites until stiff peaks form. Fold gently but thoroughly into pudding mixture. Place one banana-topped cake on decorative plate. Spoon half of the pudding mixture evenly over bananas. Sprinkle lightly with nutmeg. Top with remaining banana-topped cake and spoon remaining pudding mixture evenly over bananas. Sprinkle lightly with nutmeg. Cover with plastic wrap and refrigerate overnight.

SERVES 10; 2 FAT GRAMS AND 12% CALORIES FROM FAT PER SERVING.

Old-Fashioned "Ice Cream" Cake Roll

A chocolate cake roll filled with frozen yogurt and lightly dusted with cocoa

1 Basic Cake Roll recipe, page 17
¼ cup plus 1 tablespoon cocoa
  powder, divided
1 teaspoon almond extract

1 teaspoon instant coffee granules
2 tablespoons hot water
3 cups frozen nonfat vanilla
  yogurt

Preheat oven to 350 degrees.

Follow the Basic Cake Roll recipe, omitting 1 tablespoon of the sugar and adding ¼ cup of the cocoa powder and the almond extract. Dissolve coffee granules in hot water and add to batter. Blend thoroughly.

Proceed with baking instructions, but dust and roll with the remaining tablespoon of cocoa powder instead of powdered sugar.

While cake is cooling, place the measured frozen yogurt in refrigerator to soften slightly, about 20–30 minutes.

When cake has cooled, gently unroll and spoon slightly softened yogurt evenly over cake. Spread carefully with a knife. Gently roll, placing seam side down. Wrap with plastic wrap and freeze until firm. Slice and serve.

SERVES 10; 2.2 FAT GRAMS AND 13% CALORIES FROM FAT PER SERVING.

Variation: Substitute ice milk for frozen nonfat yogurt—3.9 fat grams and 23% calories from fat per serving.

Raspberry-Berry Jelly Roll

A delicate cake roll lined with raspberry spread and fresh strawberry slices, rolled and covered with a light whipped topping

1 Basic Cake Roll recipe, page 17

⅔ cup low-calorie raspberry
  spread

2½ cups thinly sliced strawberries

1½ cups light whipped topping

Preheat oven to 350 degrees.

Follow the Basic Cake Roll recipe and roll in towel. When cake has cooled completely, gently unroll. Spoon raspberry spread evenly over unrolled cake. Arrange strawberry slices on top and gently roll, placing seam side down. Spread whipped topping evenly over cake roll, cover with plastic wrap, and refrigerate overnight or at least 4 hours.

SERVES 10; 3.2 FAT GRAMS AND 19% CALORIES FROM FAT PER SERVING.

SWEETNESS AND LIGHT COCONUT CAKE ROLL

A delicate cake roll filled with a light vanilla and coconut whipped frosting

1 Basic Cake Roll recipe, page 17
2 egg whites, room temperature
¼ teaspoon cream of tartar

2 teaspoons vanilla extract
¼ cup granulated sugar
¾ cup flaked sweetened coconut

Preheat oven to 350 degrees.

Follow the Basic Cake Roll recipe, omitting 2 tablespoons of the sugar in batter. Dust with the 2 tablespoons powdered sugar and roll. In a small nonplastic bowl, using an electric mixer on high speed, beat egg whites with cream of tartar and vanilla extract until soft peaks form. Gradually add sugar, 1 tablespoon at a time, and beat until stiff peaks form, being careful not to overbeat. Gently fold in coconut. When cake has cooled, unroll and spread coconut mixture over cake. Gently roll, placing seam side down. Refrigerate until time of serving.

SERVES 10; 4.2 FAT GRAMS AND 25% CALORIES FROM FAT PER SERVING.

CHEESECAKE WITH A CHOCOLATE RASPBERRY BASE

Cheesecake baked with raspberry candies or kirsch and lined in chocolate cookie crumbs

1¾ cups nonfat cottage cheese	¼ teaspoon almond extract
8 ounces Neufchâtel cheese	½ teaspoon lemon zest
¼ cup skim milk	2 egg whites, room temperature
⅓ cup granulated sugar, divided	8 chocolate wafers, crushed
½ cup egg substitute	8 raspberry-filled hard candies *or*
2 teaspoons vanilla extract	3 tablespoons kirsch liqueur

Preheat oven to 275 degrees.

Place cottage cheese, Neufchâtel cheese, and milk in food processor. Blend until smooth and creamy. Add ¼ cup of the sugar, egg substitute, vanilla and almond extracts, and lemon zest. Blend until smooth.

In a separate bowl, using an electric mixer on high speed, beat egg whites until soft peaks form. Gradually add remaining sugar and beat until stiff peaks form. Gently fold egg whites into cream cheese mixture and set aside.

Coat a 9-inch springform pan with low-calorie cooking spray. Line bottom of pan with cookie crumbs. Arrange hard candies evenly on top of cookie crumbs *or* slowly drizzle kirsch over crumbs. Carefully pour batter over all.

Bake for one hour. Turn oven off and allow cake to remain in oven 30 minutes longer. Remove from oven. (Cheesecake will become firm during cooling process.) Place on wire rack and cool to room temperature. Refrigerate overnight or at least 4 hours.

SERVES 10; 4.4 FAT GRAMS AND 26% CALORIES FROM FAT PER SERVING.

CHEESECAKE FRANGELICO

A luscious, light, no-bake cheesecake topped with peaches and a hint of hazelnut

Butter-flavored low-calorie cooking spray
2 phyllo leaves
8 ounces nonfat cream cheese
¼ cup granulated sugar
1 cup light sour cream

2 tablespoons hazelnut liqueur, divided
1 8-ounce container light whipped topping
2 cups thinly sliced peaches

Preheat oven to 350 degrees.

Coat a 9-inch springform pan with low-calorie cooking spray. Cut 2 phyllo sheets in quarters and place in pie pan overlapping each other. Spray with cooking spray. Press gently to fit bottom of pan and tuck edges under a bit to form a ruffled appearance. Bake 4–6 minutes or until golden. Cool.

In large mixing bowl, using an electric mixer on high speed, beat cream cheese until light and fluffy; beat in sugar until well blended. Add sour cream and 1 tablespoon of the liqueur. Blend thoroughly, scraping bottom and sides of bowl, until smooth and creamy in texture. Gently but thoroughly, using a rubber spatula, fold in light whipped topping. Carefully spoon into baked phyllo crust and spread evenly. Chill 4 hours.

In small bowl, add sliced peaches and the remaining tablespooon of liqueur. Toss thoroughly and refrigerate overnight, or at least 1 hour.

At time of serving, remove sides of pan, slice, and place on individual dessert plates. Spoon approximately 3–4 tablespoons of the peach mixture on or around each serving.

SERVES 10; 3 FAT GRAMS AND 18% CALORIES FROM FAT PER SERVING.

CRUSTLESS CHEESECAKE WITH FRESH BLUEBERRY SAUCE

Cheesecake loaded with flavor minus the guilt

1¾ cups nonfat cottage cheese
8 ounces Neufchâtel cheese
¼ cup skim milk
½ cup plus 1 teaspoon granulated sugar, divided
2 teaspoons vanilla extract

½ teaspoon grated lemon rind
½ cup egg substitute
2 egg whites, room temperature
1 cup blueberries
2 tablespoons water

Preheat oven to 275 degrees.

In food processor, combine cottage cheese, Neufchâtel cheese, and milk. Blend until smooth. Add ⅓ cup of the sugar, vanilla extract, grated lemon rind, and egg substitute. Process until very smooth.

In separate nonplastic bowl, using electric mixer on high speed, beat egg whites until soft peaks form. Gradually add 2 tablespoons of the sugar, 1 tablespoon at a time, reserving the last tablespoon for later use, and beat until stiff peaks form. Gently fold egg whites into cheese mixture.

Coat a 9-inch springform pan with a low-calorie cooking spray. Pour batter into pan and bake 1 hour. Turn off oven and allow cake to remain in oven 30 minutes longer.

Remove from oven. (Cheesecake will become firm during cooling process.) Place on wire rack and cool to room temperature. Refrigerate overnight or at least 4 hours.

Toss blueberries and water with the remaining tablespoon of sugar and refrigerate 4 hours.

At time of serving, spoon about 2 tablespoons of sauce over each serving.

SERVES 10; 3.8 FAT GRAMS AND 23% CALORIES FROM FAT PER SERVING.

Layered Chocolate-Chocolate and Sweet Black Cherries

Layers of chocolate cookie crumbs, fresh sweet cherries, and a no-bake chocolate cheesecake filling

4 ounces nonfat cream cheese, softened

2 tablespoons powdered sugar

1 tablespoon plus 1½ teaspoons cocoa powder

¼ teaspoon instant coffee granules

1 tablespoon hot water

½ cup light vanilla yogurt

¼ teaspoon vanilla extract

⅛ teaspoon almond extract

1¾ cups (4 ounces) light whipped topping

14 chocolate wafers, crushed

18 fresh black cherries, halved and pitted, plus 6 whole cherries with stems on

With electric mixer on high speed, beat cream cheese until fluffy. Beat in sugar and cocoa powder until thoroughly blended.

Dissolve coffee granules in the hot water and add to cream cheese mixture along with yogurt and vanilla and almond extracts. Blend until smooth and creamy. Gently but thoroughly fold in whipped topping.

Place half of the cookie crumbs on bottom of glass or decorative bowl. Arrange half of the cherries evenly over crumbs. Gently spoon half of the cream cheese mixture evenly over cherries. Repeat layers of each, reserving 2 tablespoons of the cookie crumbs. Mound whole cherries in center and sprinkle with reserved cookie crumbs. Chill overnight.

SERVES 6; 4.8 FAT GRAMS AND 28% CALORIES FROM FAT PER SERVING.

The Common Comforts—
Quick Breads, Snack
Cakes, Puddings, and More

Fresh Blueberry-Lemon Muffins

Warm and sweet, perfect for any time of the day or night

1 cup fresh *or* frozen blueberries,
thawed and well drained

2 cups all-purpose flour, divided

2 teaspoons baking powder

1 teaspoon baking soda

¼ teaspoon salt

½ cup plus 2 tablespoons
granulated sugar

1 cup skim milk

¼ cup egg substitute

¼ cup unsweetened applesauce

2 tablespoons vegetable oil

1 teaspoon vanilla extract

1 tablespoon plus 2 teaspoons
grated lemon rind

1 tablespoon powdered sugar,
optional

Preheat oven to 400 degrees.

Coat a nonstick 12-muffin tin with low-calorie spray. Toss blueberries with 2 tablespoons flour and set aside.

In mixing bowl, combine remaining flour, baking powder, baking soda, and salt. Blend well.

Combine granulated sugar, milk, egg substitute, applesauce, oil, and vanilla extract. Mix thoroughly.

Make a well in center of dry ingredients and pour milk mixture in center; add lemon rind. Using a wooden spoon, gently mix together just until blended. Batter will be lumpy. Gently fold in blueberries. Spoon even amounts of batter in each tin.

Bake 18–20 minutes or until wooden pick inserted comes out clean.

Immediately remove from tins. If desired, sift 1 tablespoon powdered sugar over all and cool slightly on wire rack. Serve warm.

SERVES 12; 2.4 FAT GRAMS AND 15% CALORIES FROM FAT PER SERVING.

Hearty and Sweet Cranberry Bread

Slices of moist cranberry and orange bread with a light, crusty cinnamon sugar topping

1 cup all-purpose flour
⅔ cup quick-cooking oats
½ cup plus 1 tablespoon granulated sugar, divided
2 teaspoons baking powder
½ teaspoon baking soda
¾ teaspoon ground cinnamon, divided

¾ cup skim milk
¼ cup egg substitute
3 tablespoons orange juice concentrate
2 tablespoons vegetable oil
½ teaspoon grated orange rind
1 cup fresh cranberries, coarsely chopped

Preheat oven to 350 degrees.

In medium mixing bowl, combine flour, oats, ½ cup of the sugar, baking powder, baking soda, and ¼ teaspoon of the cinnamon. Mix thoroughly. Make a well in center of dry ingredients. Combine milk, egg substitute, orange juice concentrate, oil, and rind. Add to dry ingredients and stir until just blended. Stir in cranberries. In small bowl, combine remaining 1 tablespoon sugar with ½ teaspoon cinnamon. Mix thoroughly.

Coat a 9-inch × 5-inch × 3-inch loaf pan with low-calorie cooking spray. Pour batter into pan, sprinkle with cinnamon sugar, and bake 55 minutes. Remove from oven and place pan on wire rack to cool.

SERVES 10; 3.3 FAT GRAMS AND 20% CALORIES FROM FAT PER SERVING.

CAKE AND "ICE CREAM" SIMPLICITY

A warm slice of devil's food snack cake accompanied by a scoop of frozen yogurt

⅔ cup all-purpose flour
¼ cup unsweetened cocoa
   powder
1½ teaspoon baking powder
⅛ teaspoon salt
½ cup plus 2 tablespoons
   granulated sugar

½ cup unsweetened applesauce
¼ cup egg substitute
2 teaspoons vanilla extract
2¼ cups frozen nonfat vanilla
   yogurt

Preheat oven to 350 degrees.

Coat a 9-inch × 9-inch baking pan with low-calorie cooking spray.

In medium mixing bowl, combine flour, cocoa powder, baking powder, and salt. Mix well. Make a well in center of dry ingredients. Whisk together sugar, applesauce, egg substitute, and vanilla extract. Pour in center of well and stir until just blended. Batter will be lumpy. Pour batter into prepared pan and bake 30 minutes. Place pan on wire rack and cool 10–15 minutes.

Serve warm with ¼ cup frozen yogurt alongside each serving.

SERVES 9; 0.4 FAT GRAM AND 3% CALORIES FROM FAT PER SERVING.

October's Pumpkin Squares

A mellow and moist snack cake delicious served hot or cold

1¼ cups all-purpose flour
⅔ cup quick-cooking rolled oats
5 tablespoons granulated sugar
1½ teaspoons baking powder
1 teaspoon baking soda
¼ teaspoon salt
2 teaspoons ground cinnamon
½ teaspoon ground nutmeg
½ teaspoon ground ginger
⅛ teaspoon ground cloves

1 teaspoon orange rind, divided
1 cup canned pumpkin
½ cup skim milk
¼ cup egg substitute
3 tablespoons vegetable oil
3 tablespoons maple syrup
2 teaspoons vanilla extract
½ cup apple juice
1½ tablespoons light brown sugar, packed

Preheat oven to 325 degrees.

Coat a 9-inch × 13-inch baking pan with low-calorie cooking spray and set aside.

In a mixing bowl, combine flour, oats, sugar, baking powder, baking soda, salt, cinnamon, nutmeg, ginger, and cloves. Mix well and set aside.

In separate bowl, combine ½ teaspoon of the orange rind, pumpkin, milk, egg substitute, oil, syrup, and vanilla extract. Blend thoroughly. Add to dry ingredients and mix until just blended.

Spoon into prepared baking pan and bake 25 minutes or until wooden pick inserted comes out clean.

While cake is baking, in a small saucepan, combine apple juice and light brown sugar. Bring to boil and continue boiling 3 minutes or until the juice boils down to measure ⅓ cup. Stir in remaining ½ teaspoon orange rind and set aside.

When cake is done, place on wire rack and spoon warm sauce over warm cake. If desired, top each serving with one tablespoon of the whipped topping.

SERVES 12; 4 FAT GRAMS AND 24% CALORIES FROM FAT PER SERVING.

Sweet Banana Snack Cake

A "quick and easy" with the flavors of home

- 1 Duncan Hines Butter Recipe Golden packaged cake mix
- ½ cup egg substitute
- ⅔ cup water
- ¾ teaspoon ground cinnamon
- ¼ teaspoon ground nutmeg
- 1 medium very ripe banana, well mashed

Preheat oven to 375 degrees.

Coat a 9-inch × 13-inch baking pan with low-calorie cooking spray and set aside.

In mixing bowl, with electric mixer on low speed, combine cake mix, egg substitute, water, cinnamon, and nutmeg. Beat, scraping bottom and sides with rubber spatula, until just moistened. Add mashed banana and beat on medium speed 4 minutes.

Pour into prepared pan and bake 28–33 minutes or until wooden pick inserted comes out clean. Let stand 15 minutes before serving. Serve warm or room temperature.

SERVES 15; 3.1 FAT GRAMS AND 18% CALORIES FROM FAT PER SERVING.

Warm Ginger and Spice Squares

A wonderful spiced snack cake served warm with whipped topping

½ cup natural unsweetened applesauce

⅓ cup light brown sugar, packed

6 tablespoons maple syrup

¼ cup egg substitute

2 teaspoons vanilla extract

1 tablespoon grated orange rind, optional

¾ cup plus 2 tablespoons all-purpose flour

1½ teaspoons baking powder

¼ teaspoon baking soda

1 teaspoon ground ginger

1 teaspoon ground cinnamon

¼ teaspoon ground nutmeg

⅛ teaspoon ground cloves

1 cup light whipped topping

Preheat oven to 350 degrees.

Coat an 8-inch × 8-inch baking pan with low-calorie cooking spray.

In mixing bowl, using an electric mixer on high speed, blend applesauce, brown sugar, syrup, egg substitute, and vanilla extract until smooth.

Combine orange rind, flour, baking powder, baking soda, ginger, cinnamon, nutmeg, and cloves. Mix well and add to creamed mixture. Stir until *just* blended.

Spoon into prepared pan and bake 20 minutes. Immediately remove from oven. Do not overbake. Cake will continue cooking while cooling. Place on wire rack. Let cool 15 minutes. Top each serving with 2 tablespoons whipped topping.

Serve warm or at room temperature.

SERVES 8; 2 FAT GRAMS AND 12% CALORIES FROM FAT PER SERVING.

Baked Homestyle Vanilla Custard

A rich yet lighter version of an old-time favorite

4 eggs, slightly beaten
½ cup granulated sugar
1 teaspoon vanilla, butter, and nut flavoring

⅛ teaspoon salt
2 cups skim milk, scalded
Nutmeg

Preheat oven to 425 degrees.

Combine eggs; sugar; vanilla, butter, and nut flavoring; and salt. Whisk together until well-blended. Gradually add milk, stirring constantly. Pour into six 6-ounce glass baking cups. Sprinkle with nutmeg. Bake 12–15 minutes or when knife inserted in center comes out clean. Remove from oven. Cool to room temperature and chill thoroughly.

SERVES 6; 3.9 FAT GRAMS AND 23% CALORIES FROM FAT PER SERVING.

Double Lemon with Blueberries and Ladyfingers

A light trifle layered with a simple lemon mousse, fresh blueberries, and delicate ladyfingers

1 3-ounce package regular instant lemon pudding mix	Juice of 2 lemons
1½ cups skim milk	2 cups light whipped topping
Grated rind of 2 lemons	8 ladyfingers, split and separated
	1 cup fresh blueberries

In a medium mixing bowl, combine pudding mix, milk, lemon rind, and lemon juice. Using an electric mixer on high speed, blend well. Fold in whipped topping.

In a 9-inch deep-dish glass pie pan, arrange half of the split ladyfingers on bottom of pan. Spoon pudding mixture on top. Arrange remaining half of the split ladyfingers in spoke fashion and place berries between spokes. Chill overnight or at least 3 hours.

SERVES 8; 3.1 FAT GRAMS AND 19% CALORIES FROM FAT PER SERVING.

Variation: *In a deep, decorative bowl, arrange in layers using half the pudding, ladyfingers, and berries; repeat layers using the other half. Chill as directed.*

Easy Old-Fashioned Banana Pudding

Mounds of comfort after a busy day

2 3-ounce packages instant
 sugar-free vanilla pudding
 mix
4½ cups skim milk
 1 teaspoon vanilla extract

2 egg whites, room temperature
25 vanilla wafers
 2 medium ripe bananas
 Nutmeg

In medium-size bowl, using an electric mixer on low speed, blend together pudding mix, skim milk, and vanilla extract until smooth.

Wash and thoroughly dry beaters. In a nonplastic small bowl, add egg whites and beat on high speed of electric mixer until stiff peaks form. Gently but thoroughly fold egg whites into pudding mixture.

In a 2-quart casserole dish, place 13 vanilla wafers on bottom of dish. Spoon half of the pudding mixture over wafers. Thinly slice and arrange 1 banana over pudding. Repeat with layer of wafers and remaining pudding. Reserve remaining banana until time of serving.

Chill overnight or at least 4 hours.

At time of serving, thinly slice and arrange remaining banana over pudding and sprinkle with nutmeg.

SERVES 10; 3.7 FAT GRAMS AND 23% CALORIES FROM FAT PER SERVING.

EGGNOG BORDEAUX

A vanilla mousse flavored with brandy and a hint of nutmeg, served with rich Bordeaux cookies

2 3-ounce packages instant regular vanilla pudding mix	4 egg whites, room temperature
2¾ cups skim milk	Nutmeg
1 tablespoon brandy	24 Pepperidge Farm Bordeaux Cookies
1 teaspoon vanilla extract	

In large mixing bowl, using an electric mixer on medium speed, blend together pudding mix with skim milk until smooth. Beat in brandy and vanilla extract.

In separate bowl, with clean beaters on high speed, beat egg whites until stiff peaks form.

Gently fold egg whites into pudding mixture. Spoon into decorative bowl or wine goblets, sprinkle with nutmeg, and chill at least 3 hours. At time of serving, place 2 cookies alongside each serving.

SERVES 12; 2.6 FAT GRAMS AND 15% CALORIES FROM FAT PER SERVING.

Old-Fashioned Apple Bread Pudding in Vanilla "Cream" Sauce

The cold winter's night comfort food

- 2 cups skim milk, scalded
- 4 cups 40-calorie bread (approximately 6 slices), cubed
- 2 large eggs, well beaten
- ¼ cup light brown sugar, packed
- 2 teaspoons vanilla, butter, and nut flavoring *or* vanilla extract
- ¼ teaspoon salt, optional
- 2 teaspoons ground cinnamon
- ½ teaspoon ground nutmeg, divided

- 1½ cups medium Red Delicious apples, peeled and sliced
- 2 tablespoons apple juice concentrate
- 2 tablespoons water
- 1 teaspoon granulated sugar
- 1 8-ounce carton low-fat vanilla yogurt

Preheat oven to 350 degrees.

In a large mixing bowl, combine milk; bread; eggs; brown sugar; vanilla, butter, and nut flavoring; salt, if desired; cinnamon; and ¼ teaspoon of the nutmeg. Stir gently but thoroughly and set aside. In a small saucepan, combine apples, apple juice concentrate, and water. Bring to a boil, reduce heat, cover tightly, and simmer 4 minutes. Gently stir apples and liquid into bread mixture and spoon into a 9-inch × 9-inch baking dish coated with low-calorie cooking spray. Bake 30 minutes. Combine granulated sugar with ¼ teaspoon nutmeg. Sprinkle over bread pudding and bake 20 minutes longer.

At time of serving, place warm bread pudding on individual dessert plates and spoon 2 tablespoons of vanilla yogurt on plate around outer edge of each bread pudding serving. Serve bread pudding warm or room temperature.

SERVES 8; 150 CALORIES, 2 FAT GRAMS, AND 12% CALORIES FROM FAT PER SERVING.

DOUBLE PINEAPPLE COFFEE CAKE

A refreshing and rich-tasting cake with pineapple cooked in and crowned with more

2 8-ounce cans crushed pineapple in heavy syrup, undrained, divided
2 teaspoons cornstarch
1⅔ cups all-purpose flour
7 tablespoons granulated sugar
1 tablespoon baking powder
½ teaspoon baking soda
¼ teaspoon salt
¼ teaspoon nutmeg
3 egg whites
2 tablespoons margarine, melted
⅓ cup plus 2 tablespoons skim milk
1 teaspoon grated orange rind
1 tablespoon vanilla extract
2 tablespoons powdered sugar

Preheat oven to 350 degrees.

In small saucepan, combine pineapple and cornstarch. Blend well. Bring to boil and boil 1 minute. Remove from heat and set aside. Combine flour, sugar, baking powder, baking soda, salt, and nutmeg. Mix together and set aside.

In separate bowl, combine egg whites, margarine, milk, grated orange rind, and vanilla extract. Using an electric mixer, beat until smooth. Blend in flour mixture; stir until just blended. Batter will appear a bit stiff.

Coat a 9-inch springform pan with a low-calorie cooking spray. Spoon half the batter into pan and spread evenly. Using a teaspoon, spoon one half of the pineapple mixture over batter. Spoon remaining batter evenly on top and top with remaining pineapple sauce. Bake 50 minutes—no longer. Remove from oven; place on wire rack to cool. (Cake will continue cooking while cooling.) When completely cooled, dust powdered sugar on top. Cover with plastic wrap. Flavor improves if allowed to stand overnight.

SERVES 12; 1.9 FAT GRAMS AND 11% CALORIES FROM FAT PER SERVING.

HIDDEN APPLE COFFEE CAKE

A delicious warm coffee cake baked with a layer of sweetened apples inside

1 cup sliced Golden Delicious
  apples, peeled
1½ teaspoons cinnamon, divided
1⅓ cups plus 2 teaspoons all-
  purpose flour, divided
½ cup granulated sugar, divided
¼ cup margarine, softened
¼ cup egg substitute
⅔ cup skim milk
1 teaspoon vanilla extract
2 teaspoons baking powder
½ teaspoon baking soda

Preheat oven to 375 degrees.

In a small bowl, combine apples, ½ teaspoon cinnamon, 2 tablespoons flour, and 2 tablespoons sugar. Toss well and set aside.

In a mixing bowl, using an electric mixer at high speed, cream margarine; add ¼ cup sugar and beat until light. Add egg substitute, milk, and vanilla extract. Beat well. Sift into creamed mixture 1¼ cups flour, baking powder, and baking soda. Blend well.

Coat a 9-inch springform pan with low-calorie cooking spray. Pour half of the batter in pan. Spoon apple mixture evenly over batter. Top with remaining half of batter. Combine remaining 2 tablespoons sugar and 1 teaspoon cinnamon and mix well. Sprinkle over cake and bake 22–25 minutes, or until wooden pick inserted comes out clean. Cool on wire rack 10 minutes.

Serve warm.

SERVES 10; 4.5 FAT GRAMS AND 27% CALORIES FROM FAT PER SERVING.

COUNTRY-STYLE STRAWBERRY SHORTCAKE

Warm, drop-style shortcakes filled with sweetened strawberries, topped with more berries and whipped topping

3 cups sliced fresh strawberries, divided

5 tablespoons granulated sugar, divided

1¾ cups all-purpose flour

1 tablespoon baking powder

¼ teaspoon salt

3 tablespoons margarine

¾ cup plus 2 tablespoons skim milk

½ cup plus 2 tablespoons light whipped topping

Preheat oven to 450 degrees.

Coat a nonstick baking sheet with low-calorie cooking spray.

In small bowl, mash ½ cup of the sliced strawberries, add remaining sliced strawberries, and 3 tablespoons of the sugar. Stir well and set aside.

Sift together flour, baking powder, salt, and remaining 2 tablespoons sugar. Cut in margarine until dough gives the appearance of coarse meal. Add milk; stir lightly with fork.

Drop by tablespoonfuls onto prepared baking sheet to make 10 mounds. Bake 7–10 minutes.

Immediately remove from oven, split crosswise, spoon approximately ¼ cup strawberry mixture on bottom half, place other half of shortcake on top, and top with approximately 2 tablespoons strawberry sauce. Place 1 tablespoon light whipped topping on each serving. Serve immediately, while still warm.

SERVES 10; 4.1 FAT GRAMS AND 24% CALORIES FROM FAT PER SERVING.

RASPBERRY-PEAR TEA CAKE

A delicate, almond-flavored tea cake covered in a colorful raspberry glaze

1 cup all-purpose flour
1 tablespoon baking powder
½ teaspoon baking soda
¼ teaspoon cinnamon
⅓ cup granulated sugar
¼ cup margarine, melted
2 egg whites
2 teaspoons almond extract

½ cup canned pears, in its own juice, drained, reserving 2 tablespoons juice
½ cup raspberries in heavy syrup, frozen and thawed
2 teaspoons cornstarch
¼ teaspoon lemon zest

Preheat oven to 350 degrees.

Combine flour, baking powder, baking soda, and cinnamon; set aside.

In a separate bowl, whisk together sugar, margarine, egg whites, and almond extract. Drain pears and reserve 2 tablespoons of pear juice. With fork, mash pears and blend with egg white mixture. Stir flour mixture in until just moistened.

Coat a 9-inch springform pan with a low-calorie cooking spray. Pour batter into pan and bake 20 minutes or until wooden pick inserted comes out clean.

While cake is baking, in small saucepan, combine raspberries, the reserved 2 tablespoons pear juice, and cornstarch. Stir until cornstarch dissolves. Bring to a boil and continue boiling 1 minute. Remove from heat to cool to room temperature. Stir in lemon zest.

When cake is done, place pan on wire rack to cool. When completely cooled, remove sides and bottom of pan. Place tea cake on decorative plate. Cover with plastic wrap until time of serving. At time of serving, spoon sauce over all.

SERVES 9; 5 FAT GRAMS AND 30% CALORIES FROM FAT PER SERVING.

The Cookie Bin

ALMOND MACAROONS

A light cookie to the touch, with a rich, chewy almond center

1 8-ounce can almond paste   1 cup granulated sugar
3 egg whites

Preheat oven to 325 degrees.

Line a baking sheet with foil.

In a medium mixing bowl, combine almond paste, egg whites, and sugar. Blend, using hands, until thoroughly mixed. Spoon by teaspoonfuls 2 inches apart, and bake 15 minutes. Place cookies and the foil on wire rack to cool.

Line baking sheet with more foil and repeat process until all batter has been used.

When cookies have cooled completely, gently remove from foil and store in airtight container.

Makes 36 cookies.

EACH 3-COOKIE SERVING CONTAINS 5.1 FAT GRAMS AND 31% CALORIES FROM FAT.

CHOCOLATE CHIP COOKIES

Deliciously butter-flavored cookies with tiny morsels of chocolate

½ cup dark brown sugar, packed
⅓ cup granulated sugar
¼ cup margarine, softened
¼ cup egg substitute
1 teaspoon vanilla, butter, and
   nut flavoring

⅔ cup all-purpose flour
2 teaspoons baking powder
½ teaspoon baking soda
¼ teaspoon salt
⅓ cup semisweet minimorsel
   chocolate chips

Preheat oven to 350 degrees.

In medium mixing bowl, combine brown sugar; granulated sugar; margarine; egg substitute; and vanilla, butter, and nut flavoring.

Using an electric mixer on high speed, cream together until smooth and fluffy.

Combine flour, baking powder, baking soda, and salt. Gradually add and mix until well blended. Fold in chocolate chips. Coat a nonstick cookie sheet with low-calorie cooking spray. Drop by level teaspoonfuls onto cookie sheet 2 inches apart and bake 9–10 minutes. Let stand one minute on cookie sheet before removing with a metal spatula. Cool on wire rack.

Makes 48 cookies.

EACH 4-COOKIE SERVING CONTAINS 5.1 FAT GRAMS AND 30% CALORIES FROM FAT.

CHOCOLATE THUMBKINS WITH FROZEN YOGURT

Deep chocolate thumbprint-type cookies filled with milk chocolate centers and served with a scoop of frozen yogurt

¼ cup margarine, softened
⅓ cup granulated sugar
2 teaspoons vanilla extract
¼ cup egg substitute
¾ cup plus 1 teaspoon all-purpose flour, divided
¼ cup cocoa powder

½ teaspoon baking soda
Flour
½ cup milk chocolate or semisweet chocolate chips
1 tablespoon plus 1 teaspoon skim milk
Frozen nonfat vanilla yogurt

Preheat oven to 350 degrees.

Using an electric mixer on high speed, cream together margarine, sugar, and vanilla extract until light and fluffy. Beat in egg substitute. Mix in ¾ cup of the flour, cocoa powder, and baking soda.

Coat a nonstick cookie sheet with low-calorie cooking spray. Drop by scant teaspoonfuls onto cookie sheet 1 inch apart. Dust thumb with remaining teaspoon of flour and press to make indentation in center of each cookie. Bake 5 minutes. Cool completely.

To make filling, in small saucepan over low heat, melt chocolate chips, smoothing with rubber spatula. When melted, add milk; blend until smooth. Remove from heat and let stand at least 3 minutes. Spoon ¼ teaspoon in center of each cookie.

Makes 55 cookies.

Place a ¼-cup scoop of frozen yogurt and 4 cookies on each dessert plate.

EACH SERVING CONTAINS 4.8 FAT GRAMS AND 29% CALORIES FROM FAT.

CRISPY ALMOND ROUNDS WITH FRESH PEACHES

Delicate, refreshing, and absolutely wonderful

1¾ cups plus 2 tablespoons all-purpose flour
1 teaspoon baking powder
¼ teaspoon salt
5 tablespoons shortening
3 tablespoons margarine, softened
½ cup plus 2 tablespoons granulated sugar, divided
6 tablespoons powdered sugar
1½ teaspoons almond extract
½ teaspoon vanilla extract
¼ cup egg substitute
½ cup (2¼ ounces) almond slices, crushed
Fresh peach slices

Preheat oven to 350 degrees.

Sift together flour, baking powder, and salt. Set aside.

In medium mixing bowl, using an electric mixer on high speed, cream together shortening, margarine, ½ cup of the granulated sugar, powdered sugar, and almond and vanilla extracts. Beat until light and fluffy. Beat in egg substitute. Gradually add flour mixture. Mix until just blended.

Separate and lightly shape into 6 balls. Place each ball on a sheet of plastic wrap. Loosely wrap and gently press each into 4-inch patties. Chill in single layers overnight or at least 1 hour.

When chilled, remove 1 patty from refrigerator and place on 18-inch sheet of plastic wrap lightly dusted with flour. Top with another sheet of plastic wrap. Quickly roll dough very thin. Cut into twelve 2-inch circles. Using metal spatula, place 1 inch apart on a nonstick cookie sheet coated with low-calorie cooking spray.

Sprinkle evenly 1 tablespoon plus 1 teaspoon of the crushed almonds on each batch. Sprinkle 1 teaspoon sugar per batch over almonds.

Bake 4–6 minutes. Remove cookies with metal spatula. Cool on wire rack. Makes 72 cookies.

Serve 3 cookies with ½ cup fresh peach slices per person.

EACH SERVING CONTAINS 5.8 FAT GRAMS AND 34% CALORIES FROM FAT.

CRUNCHY TOFFEE CANDY COOKIES WITH FROZEN PEACH YOGURT

Butter-rich, lacy cookies to be loved by kids of all ages

½ cup (2 ounces) pecan pieces
½ cup all-purpose flour
⅓ cup butter (not margarine)*
½ cup light brown sugar, packed

¼ cup light corn syrup
½ teaspoon vanilla, butter, and nut flavoring
Frozen nonfat peach yogurt

Preheat oven to 375 degrees.

In processor, combine pecans and flour until coarse meal texture and set aside.

In small saucepan, combine butter, sugar, and corn syrup. Bring to full boil and stir well. Remove from heat. Add pecan mixture and vanilla, butter, and nut flavoring; stir well.

Liberally coat 2 nonstick cookie sheets with low-calorie cooking spray. By half teaspoonfuls, spoon batter for 6 cookies on 1 cookie sheet 3 inches apart.

Bake exactly 4 minutes. While cookies are baking, spoon batter on other cookie sheet.

When cookies have baked 4 minutes, immediately remove from oven. They will have a very light color and not appear to be done; they will continue cooking after being removed from oven. Let stand exactly 1 minute before removing from cookie sheet. Using a metal spatula, gently but quickly remove cookies and place on wire rack to cool.

* Be sure to use butter, not margarine. Margarine does not allow cookies to spread properly.

Note: Midway through preparation and baking, warm batter over low heat to ensure easy handling and correct baking time. Repeat procedure, coating with cooking spray each time, until all batter has been used. Makes 60 cookies total. Store in airtight container.

Serve 3 cookies with ⅓-cup scoop of frozen peach yogurt per person.

EACH SERVING CONTAINS 4.3 FAT GRAMS AND 26% CALORIES FROM FAT.

Delicate Orange Cookies with Creamy Fruit Compote

Light and mildly flavored orange cookies served with green grapes tossed with sweet vanilla yogurt

½ cup margarine, softened
½ cup plus 2 tablespoons granulated sugar
¼ cup egg substitute
2 teaspoons vanilla extract
1 cup plus 3 tablespoons all-purpose flour
½ teaspoon baking soda
¼ teaspoon ground nutmeg
¼ teaspoon salt
1 tablespoon grated orange rind
2 tablespoons orange juice concentrate
1 teaspoon lemon juice
Seedless green grapes, halved
Nonfat vanilla yogurt

Preheat oven to 350 degrees.

Coat a nonstick cookie sheet with low-calorie cooking spray.

Cream margarine and sugar well; add egg substitute and vanilla extract and beat until smooth.

Combine flour, baking soda, nutmeg, and salt. Mix well. Gradually add to creamed mixture until just blended. Blend in orange rind, orange juice concentrate, and lemon juice.

Spoon by teaspoonfuls 2 inches apart. Bake 8 minutes or until edges just begin to brown. Remove with metal spatula and cool completely on wire rack. Makes 52 cookies.

At time of serving, combine ⅓ cup halved grapes with ¼ cup light yogurt per serving. Serve in a dessert cup along with 3 cookies.

Store any remaining cookies in airtight container.

EACH SERVING CONTAINS 5.1 FAT GRAMS AND 30% CALORIES FROM FAT.

LEMON WAFERS WITH RASPBERRY DRIZZLES

Delicate lemon cookies, delicious with or without raspberry drizzles

⅓ cup margarine, softened
⅔ cup granulated sugar
1 teaspoon vanilla extract
½ teaspoon lemon extract
¼ cup egg substitute
¾ cup all-purpose flour

1 tablespoon grated lemon rind
3 tablespoons regular raspberry preserves, not low-sugar raspberry spread
Powdered sugar

Preheat oven to 350 degrees.

Coat a nonstick cookie sheet with low-calorie cooking spray.

Using an electric mixer on high speed, in medium bowl, combine margarine, sugar, and vanilla and lemon extracts. Cream until light and fluffy. Beat in egg substitute until well blended. Gradually add flour and lemon rind. Blend well.

Drop by rounded teaspoonfuls 2 inches apart. Using back of spoon, flatten center to make an even cookie. Bake 9 minutes. (Edges should not begin to brown.) Remove from oven and let stand on cookie sheet 2 minutes. Using a metal spatula, carefully remove cookies and cool completely on wire rack. Repeat process, coating cookie sheet with cooking spray each time.

When cookies have completely cooled, heat raspberry preserves in a small saucepan over low heat. Sift powdered sugar over cookies and drizzle each cookie with ¼ teaspoon of heated preserves.

When cooled, store in an airtight container. Makes 33 cookies.

EACH 3-COOKIE SERVING CONTAINS 5.4 FAT GRAMS AND 32% CALORIES FROM FAT.

Light Coconut Kisses with Fresh Pineapple and Citrus

Naturally sweetened fruits accompanied by rich and moist coconut macaroons

1⅓ cups (3½ ounces) canned
    sweetened coconut
1 tablespoon granulated sugar
3 tablespoons all-purpose flour
⅛ teaspoon salt
2 egg whites
½ teaspoon vanilla *or* almond
    extract

1 grapefruit, sectioned
1 navel orange, sectioned
1 cup fresh pineapple, cut in
    1-inch pieces
1 cup seedless red grapes
1 can diet ginger ale

Preheat oven to 325 degrees.

Line a cookie sheet with foil; coat foil with low-calorie cooking spray.

In mixing bowl, combine coconut, sugar, flour, salt, egg whites, and extract. Blend thoroughly. Drop by rounded teaspoonfuls onto lined cookie sheet, 1 inch apart. Bake 9 cookies at a time. Bake 16 minutes or until just beginning to brown. Immediately remove cookies *with* foil and place on wire rack to cool completely. Repeat baking procedure with remaining batter. Makes 18 cookies total.

When cookies have completely cooled, remove from foil. Store in airtight container.

At time of serving, combine grapefruit, oranges, pineapple, and grapes. Toss gently. Place in 6 individual dessert cups and pour ¼ cup ginger ale over each serving of fruit. Serve immediately along with 3 cookies per serving.

One serving equals ½ cup fruit with 3 cookies.

SERVES 6; 5.5 FAT GRAMS AND 33% CALORIES FROM FAT PER SERVING.

LITTLE LEMON MUDDLES

A thumbprint-type cookie with a delightful lemon pie filling

- ¼ cup margarine, softened
- ½ cup plus 1 tablespoon granulated sugar, divided
- 1 teaspoon vanilla extract
- ¼ cup plus 2 tablespoons egg substitute, divided
- ¾ cup plus 2 tablespoons all-purpose flour
- ½ teaspoon baking soda
- 1 tablespoon plus 1 teaspoon grated lemon rind, divided
- ½ cup cold water
- 1 tablespoon cornstarch
- 2 tablespoons lemon juice
- ¼ teaspoon Molly McButter
- 1–2 drops yellow food coloring
- 2 teaspoons powdered sugar

Preheat oven to 350 degrees.

Using an electric mixer on high speed, cream together margarine, ¼ cup of the sugar, and vanilla extract until light and fluffy. Beat in ¼ cup of the egg substitute. Mix in flour, soda, and 1 tablespoon of the lemon rind.

Coat a nonstick cookie sheet with low-calorie cooking spray. Drop by scant teaspoonfuls onto cookie sheet 1 inch apart. Dust thumb with flour; press to make indentation in center of each cookie. Bake 7 minutes. Cool completely.

To make filling, in small saucepan, combine the remaining ¼ cup plus 1 tablespoon sugar, water, cornstarch, lemon juice, and remaining 2 tablespoons egg substitute. Stir well until cornstarch dissolves. Bring to a boil, reduce heat, and simmer until filling thickens; stir with a flat spatula. Remove from heat. Stir in remaining 1 teaspoon lemon rind, Molly McButter, and food coloring.

Let stand 3 minutes. Spoon ¼ teaspoon in center of each cookie. Sift powdered sugar over all. Refrigerate in airtight container.

Makes 60 cookies.

EACH 7-COOKIE SERVING CONTAINS 5.1 FAT GRAMS AND 31% CALORIES FROM FAT.

Sugared Sugar Cookies

Crispy and light and straight from the oven

¾ cup plus 1 teaspoon
  granulated sugar, divided
7 tablespoons plus 1 teaspoon
  margarine, softened
2 teaspoons vanilla extract

¼ cup egg substitute
2 cups all-purpose flour
1 teaspoon baking powder
¼ teaspoon salt

Preheat oven to 400 degrees.

Using an electric mixer on high speed, cream together 9 tablespoons plus 1 teaspoon sugar, margarine, and vanilla extract until light and fluffy. Beat in egg substitute. Gradually mix in flour, baking powder, and salt. Form dough into 6 balls, cover with plastic wrap, and chill overnight or at least 1 hour.

When chilled, remove 1 ball from refrigerator and place on 18-inch sheet of plastic wrap lightly dusted with flour. Top with another sheet of plastic wrap. Quickly roll dough very thin; cut into twelve 2-inch circles, and place 1 inch apart on nonstick cookie sheet coated with low-calorie cooking spray. Sprinkle with 1½ teaspoons of the sugar. Bake 4–6 minutes. Place on wire rack to cool. Repeat process with remaining balls of dough.

Store in airtight container.

Makes 72 cookies.

EACH 5-COOKIE SERVING CONTAINS 5.5 FAT GRAMS AND 33% CALORIES FROM FAT.

Variation: *Substitute 3 tablespoons sugar reserved for tops of cookies with 72 (about 1 ounce) cinnamon hearts or red hots. Place one in center of each cookie.*

Summer's Sweet Lemon "Ice Cream" Sandwiches

Delicate lemon cookies filled with frozen vanilla yogurt

½ cup unsalted whipped butter, softened
⅔ cup granulated sugar
2 teaspoons grated lemon rind
1 large egg
3 tablespoons lemon juice
¼ teaspoon vanilla extract
¼ teaspoon salt
¾ cup all-purpose flour
4 cups frozen nonfat vanilla yogurt

Preheat oven to 350 degrees.

In a medium bowl, using an electric mixer on high speed, cream together butter, sugar, and lemon rind. Blend well. Add egg, lemon juice, vanilla extract, salt, and flour. Mix until just blended. Liberally coat nonstick cookie sheet with low-calorie cooking spray. Place rounded tea-spoonfuls of batter 2 inches apart. Using back of spoon, spread to make 3-inch circles. Makes 32 cookies. Bake 9–10 minutes or until edges begin to brown. Remove from oven. Let stand 2 minutes on cookie sheet before removing. (Cookies will continue to bake.) Place on wire rack and cool completely. Spoon ¼ cup frozen yogurt on 16 of the cookies. Top with remaining 16 cookies to form individual round ice cream sandwiches.

Serve immediately or wrap in plastic wrap and freeze until serving.

SERVES 16; 5 FAT GRAMS AND 30% CALORIES FROM FAT PER SERVING.

Sweet Frozen Taco Cookies

Crispy pecan and brown sugar wafer cookies, taco-shaped and filled with frozen yogurt, topped with lightly sweetened peaches

3 tablespoons dark brown sugar
1 egg white
1 tablespoon margarine, melted and cooled slightly
½ teaspoon vanilla extract
¼ cup (1 ounce) pecan pieces
1 tablespoon all-purpose flour

¼ teaspoon ground cinnamon
¼ teaspoon ground nutmeg
1½ cups frozen nonfat vanilla yogurt
1½ cups fresh peach slices
1 tablespoon powdered sugar

Preheat oven to 375 degrees.

In a small mixing bowl, combine sugar, egg white, margarine, and vanilla extract. Using an electric mixer on medium speed, blend well and set aside.

In processor, combine pecans and flour. Process until pecans are finely chopped. Add to brown sugar mixture along with cinnamon and nutmeg. Mix until smooth. Let stand 10 minutes.

Liberally coat a nonstick cookie sheet with low-calorie cooking spray. Stir batter. Spoon batter for only 2 cookies at a time on cookie sheet. Drop 1 tablespoon of batter on cookie sheet; using back of spoon, spread to make a 5-inch-diameter circle, repeat for other cookie and bake 5–6 minutes or until edges begin to brown slightly. Remove from oven. Let stand on cookie sheet 1–1½ minutes. Quickly but carefully remove with a metal spatula and very gently fold over to give the shape of a taco shell. Cool 5 minutes. (Another method is to balance a wooden spoon between 2 glasses and drape warm cookie over handle of spoon. Cool 5 minutes before removing.)

Repeat process with remaining batter, coating sheet with cooking spray each time. (Be sure to alternate cookie sheets, or wait until cookie sheet is completely cool for consistency.)

After cookies have cooled 5 minutes, gently fill each taco cookie with ¼ cup softened frozen yogurt. Wrap individually with plastic wrap and place in freezer until time of serving.

In medium bowl, combine peach slices and powdered sugar. Toss well and let stand at least 10 minutes.

At time of serving, spoon ¼ cup of the peach mixture on top of frozen yogurt filling for each cookie.

Serve immediately.

SERVES 6; 3.1 FAT GRAMS AND 19% CALORIES FROM FAT PER SERVING.

Variation: Simply place whole taco cookie open (*unfolded*) on dessert plate. Spoon frozen yogurt on top and spoon sweetened peaches over yogurt. Serve immediately.

SWEETUMS

Easy miniature ice cream cookies

1½ cup frozen nonfat vanilla or   24   chocolate wafers
     chocolate yogurt

Place 2 level tablespoons of frozen yogurt between 2 chocolate wafers and gently press down. Wrap in plastic wrap and freeze until time of serving. Repeat process to make 12 ice cream cookies.

SERVES 6 (2 ICE CREAM COOKIES PER SERVING); 3.2 FAT GRAMS AND 19% CALORIES FROM FAT PER SERVING.

Variation: *Substitute vanilla or chocolate ice milk for yogurt. Each serving contains approximately 4.6 fat grams and 28% calories from fat.*

WARM OATMEAL, RAISIN, AND SPICE COOKIES

Oatmeal cookies filled with plumped raisins and richly flavored seasonings

¾ cup boiling water
¾ cup raisins
7 tablespoons margarine, softened
⅔ cup granulated sugar
⅓ cup dark brown sugar, packed
¼ cup egg substitute
2 tablespoons skim milk
1 teaspoon vanilla, butter, and nut flavoring

¾ cup plus 2 tablespoons all-purpose flour
½ teaspoon baking soda
½ teaspoon ground cinnamon
½ teaspoon ground nutmeg
⅛ teaspoon salt
1¼ cups quick-cooking oats

Preheat oven to 350 degrees.

Coat cookie sheet with low-calorie spray.

In small bowl, combine water and raisins. Set aside.

In medium mixing bowl, using an electric mixer on high speed, cream margarine, granulated sugar, and brown sugar. Beat in egg substitute; skim milk; and vanilla, butter, and nut flavoring. Beat until smooth.

Combine flour, baking soda, cinnamon, nutmeg, and salt. Stir well. Beat into creamed mixture.

Drain raisins well, add raisins and oats to mixture, and mix until just blended. Spoon by teaspoonfuls about 2 inches apart.

Bake 9 minutes. Carefully remove cookies, using a metal spatula and cool slightly on wire rack. Cookies will become more firm while cooling.

Serve warm or at room temperature.

Makes 51 cookies.

EACH 3-COOKIE SERVING CONTAINS 4.9 FAT GRAMS AND 29% CALORIES FROM FAT.

The Frozens

BERRY ORANGE ICE

Fresh strawberries blended with orange and cranberry juices to create a lightly sweetened ice brimming with flavor

3 cups sliced strawberries
2 cups orange juice
1 cup low-calorie cranberry juice
2 teaspoons grated orange rind

½ cup hot water
¼ cup plus 1 tablespoon granulated sugar

Place strawberries, orange juice, cranberry juice, and orange rind in processor. Process until smooth. In small bowl, combine hot water and sugar. Stir until sugar dissolves and add to ingredients in processor. Process until well blended.

Pour into a 9-inch × 13-inch glass baking pan, cover with plastic wrap, and freeze at least 3 hours, stirring every hour until frozen.

At time of serving, remove from freezer and let stand 10 minutes. Break up in pieces and blend in processor or shave with fork. Spoon into 4 dessert dishes or wine goblets.

SERVES 4; 0.5 FAT GRAM AND 3% CALORIES FROM FAT PER SERVING.

Variation: *Process 1 cup sliced banana and an additional 1 cup strawberry slices. Add to strawberry mixture. Serves 5; 0.6 fat gram and 4% calories from fat per serving.*

FRESH KIWI ICE

Frozen slush of sweet kiwis with a hint of lime

6 ripe kiwis, peeled and quartered
3 cups water

7 tablespoons granulated sugar
1 tablespoon lime juice

Place all ingredients in processor; blend until smooth. Pour into 9-inch × 9-inch glass baking pan, cover with plastic wrap, and place in freezer at least 3 hours, stirring every hour until frozen.

At time of serving, remove from freezer and let stand 10 minutes. Shave, if necessary, with fork and spoon into 4 dessert dishes. Serve immediately.

SERVES 4; 0.1 FAT GRAM AND 0% CALORIES FROM FAT PER SERVING.

GRAPE-WINE ICE

A cool pleasure of frozen mild fruit juices, dry white wine, and ginger ale

3 cups purple grape juice	3 tablespoons lime juice
3 cups dry white wine	1 teaspoon grated lime rind
1⅓ cups diet ginger ale	4 lime wedges for garnish

Combine all ingredients except the lime wedges in a 9-inch × 13-inch glass baking pan. Stir well. Cover with plastic wrap and place in freezer for at least 3 hours, stirring every hour until frozen.

At time of serving, remove from freezer and let stand 10 minutes. Break up in pieces and blend in processor or shave with fork. Place in 6 dessert dishes or wine goblets. Garnish with lime wedges, if desired, and serve.

SERVES 6; 0.1 FAT GRAM AND 0% CALORIES FROM FAT PER SERVING.

Mexican Ice

A margarita in its mildest form

- 1 6-ounce can frozen limeade concentrate
- 1 cup water
- ¾ cup orange juice
- 2½ cups ice cubes (approximately 18 cubes)

- 2 tablespoons plus 1 teaspoon granulated sugar
- 4 orange slices for garnish

Place limeade concentrate, water, orange juice, ice cubes, and sugar in blender. Blend until smooth. Pour into 4 wine goblets or glasses and garnish with orange slices. Serve immediately or place in freezer 1 hour.

SERVES 4; 0.1 FAT GRAM AND 0% CALORIES FROM FAT PER SERVING.

PINEAPPLE, APRICOT, ORANGE, RUM SLUSH

A very cold, very refreshing frozen blend of tropical fruit juices

1 cup unsweetened pineapple juice, divided
2 tablespoons granulated sugar
3 tablespoons rum, optional
1 cup apricot nectar

1 cup orange juice
1 tablespoon plus 1½ teaspoons lime juice
1–2 teaspoons grated orange rind
4 orange slices for garnish

In small saucepan, combine ½ cup of the pineapple juice, granulated sugar, and rum, if desired. Stir well, bring to a boil, continue boiling 1 minute. Stir to dissolve sugar. Pour into 9-inch × 9-inch glass baking pan. Add apricot nectar, orange juice, lime juice, orange rind, and remaining ½ cup of the pineapple juice. Stir until well blended. Cover with plastic wrap and place in freezer. Stir every hour for 3 hours or until firm.

At time of serving, remove from freezer and let stand 10 minutes. If frozen too hard, break up in chunks with fork and place in processor; blend until smooth and pour into wine goblets. Garnish each goblet with an orange slice.

SERVES 4; 0.2 FAT GRAM AND 1% CALORIES FROM FAT PER SERVING.

Sangria Ice

A sensational blend of sweet citrus and red wine

3 cups dry red wine
2¾ cups orange juice
2 cups diet ginger ale

½ cup granulated sugar
2 tablespoons lemon juice
2 tablespoons lime juice

Combine all ingredients in a 9-inch × 13-inch glass baking pan. Stir well until sugar dissolves. Cover with plastic wrap and place in freezer for at least 3 hours, stirring every hour until frozen.

At time of serving, remove from freezer and let stand 10 minutes. Break up in pieces and blend in processor or shave ice with fork and serve in wine goblets, if desired.

SERVES 8; 0.2 FAT GRAM AND 1% CALORIES FROM FAT PER SERVING.

FROZEN CREAMY PINEAPPLE ORANGE COOLER

A creamy, lightly sweetened pineapple and orange soft frozen treat

2 cups unsweetened pineapple
juice
1 cup nonfat buttermilk
½ cup orange juice

3 tablespoons plus 2 teaspoons
granulated sugar
1 teaspoon grated orange rind

In processor, combine all ingredients and blend thoroughly. Pour into 9-inch glass baking dish, cover with plastic wrap, and freeze until firm, but not frozen solid (about 3 hours), stirring every hour until frozen. At time of serving, remove from freezer and let stand 15 minutes. Break up in pieces and blend in processor. If dessert is a bit icy, simply process or stir to dissolve crystals.

Spoon into wine goblets and serve immediately.

SERVES 4; 0.7 FAT GRAM AND 4% CALORIES FROM FAT PER SERVING.

FROZEN PINEAPPLE AND COCONUT "CREAM"

A creamy slush enjoyed by itself or with a spoon

4 cups light vanilla yogurt
1 8-ounce can crushed pineapple
  in its own juice

2 teaspoons rum, optional
1 teaspoon coconut extract
1 teaspoon vanilla extract

Place all ingredients in processor. Blend until smooth, pour into 4 wine goblets, cover with plastic wrap, and freeze 1 hour. Stir well. Serve or freeze an additional hour and process before serving.

SERVES 4; 0.1 FAT GRAM AND 0% CALORIES FROM FAT PER SERVING.

DECADENT CHOCOLATE MINT PIE

A frozen yogurt pie topped with layers of crushed peppermint candies, chocolate cookie crumbs, and grated semisweet chocolate

4 cups frozen nonfat vanilla *or* chocolate yogurt, slightly softened
1 teaspoon peppermint extract
6 hard peppermint candies, crushed

7 chocolate wafers, crushed
2 tablespoons grated semisweet chocolate

Spoon frozen yogurt evenly over bottom of 9-inch pie pan. Sprinkle peppermint extract over yogurt, spread evenly using back of spoon, top with crushed peppermints. Cover with plastic wrap and place in freezer until firm, about 1–2 hours. Sprinkle crushed wafers over crushed peppermint and top with grated chocolate.

Serve immediately or return to freezer until time of serving.

SERVES 8; 1.5 FAT GRAMS AND 9% CALORIES FROM FAT PER SERVING.

Variation: *Substitute vanilla* or *chocolate ice milk for frozen yogurt. Each serving contains approximately 4.3 fat grams, and 27% calories from fat.*

Lazy Day Banana Split Pie

A frozen vanilla yogurt pie topped with freshly sliced bananas and drizzles of rich chocolate sauce

4 graham crackers
2 tablespoons diet margarine, melted and cooled slightly
3 cups frozen nonfat vanilla yogurt, slightly softened

1 ounce semisweet chocolate chips
3 tablespoons skim milk
1½ cups sliced bananas

Preheat oven to 400 degrees.

In processor, add crackers and process to crumbs. Slowly pour melted margarine down tube of processor while blending.

Coat a 9-inch pie pan with low-calorie cooking spray. With back of spoon, press crumb mixture evenly over bottom of pie pan. Bake 4 minutes. Cool completely on wire rack.

Spoon slightly softened frozen yogurt on top and smooth to cover evenly. Cover with plastic wrap and place in freezer until firm, about 1–2 hours.

While freezing, in small saucepan over low heat, melt chocolate chips, using a rubber spatula to blend smooth. Add milk. Blend well. When smooth, remove from heat and let stand to room temperature.

At time of serving, arrange bananas on top of frozen yogurt and drizzle chocolate sauce over all.

Serve immediately, freezing any remaining portions for later use.

SERVES 8; 2.9 FAT GRAMS AND 17% CALORIES FROM FAT PER SERVING.

Variation: *Substitute ice milk for frozen yogurt. Each serving contains 5 fat grams and 30% calories from fat.*

Strawberry, Blueberry, Peach Summer Pie

A frozen vanilla yogurt pie covered with a layer of fresh strawberry sauce and topped with rings of the season's freshest fruits

4 graham crackers
2 tablespoons diet margarine, melted
3½ cups frozen nonfat vanilla yogurt, slightly softened
1 cup sliced strawberries, divided

1 tablespoon plus 1 teaspoon low-sugar strawberry spread
1 cup blueberries
1 cup sliced ripe peaches

Preheat oven to 400 degrees.

In processor, add crackers and process to crumbs. Slowly pour melted margarine down tube of processor while blending.

Coat a 9-inch pie pan with low-calorie cooking spray. With back of spoon, press crumb mixture evenly over bottom of pie pan. Bake 4 minutes. Cool completely on wire rack.

When pie crust has cooled, spoon slightly softened frozen yogurt on top and smooth to cover evenly. Cover in plastic wrap and place in freezer until firm, at least 2 hours. In a processor, combine ¾ cup of the strawberries and strawberry spread. Process to pureed texture. Refrigerate until time of serving.

At time of serving, spoon sauce evenly over frozen yogurt and decoratively arrange a ring of blueberries around the outer edge of pie, arrange peaches in smaller ring, pile remaining ¼ cup strawberry slices in center, and serve immediately, freezing any remaining portions for later use.

SERVES 8; 2.6 FAT GRAMS AND 16% CALORIES FROM FAT PER SERVING.

Variation: *Substitute 3½ cups ice milk for frozen yogurt. Each serving contains 5 fat grams and 30% calories from fat.*

DOUBLE-DIPPED FAT-FREE GOURMET "ICE CREAM" CONE

A generous serving of frozen chocolate yogurt richly flavored with mocha and almonds

¼ cup cold water
1 tablespoon instant coffee granules
½ teaspoon almond extract

2⅔ cups frozen nonfat chocolate yogurt, slightly softened
4 ice cream cones

In a medium mixing bowl, combine water, instant coffee granules, and almond extract. Stir well until granules dissolve. Gently but quickly fold coffee mixture into yogurt and freeze in bowl until firm, about 1–2 hours.

At time of serving, scoop two ⅓-cup scoops of the frozen yogurt into each of 4 ice cream cones to form 2 dips each. Serve immediately.

SERVES 4; 0 FAT GRAMS AND 0% CALORIES FROM FAT.

Variation: May substitute ice milk for frozen yogurt. Each serving contains 3.8 fat grams and 23% calories from fat.

FROZEN CHOCOLATE PUDDLES

Chocolate semisweet puddles with mocha mousse and crowned with crumbled chocolate

1 teaspoon shortening	1 teaspoon instant coffee granules
1½ ounces semisweet chocolate	1 tablespoon hot water
1 3-ounce package instant sugar-free chocolate pudding	2 egg whites, room temperature
2 cups skim milk	5 chocolate wafers, crushed

In small saucepan over low heat, melt shortening. Add chocolate and stir using rubber spatula, until melted and smooth. On five 6-inch sheets of waxed paper, spoon equal amounts of chocolate sauce. Using back of spoon, spread each into a 4-inch-diameter circle. Freeze until time of serving.

In mixing bowl, combine pudding mix with milk and stir until smooth and well blended.

In cup, dissolve coffee granules in hot water and fold into pudding mixture. In a small nonplastic bowl, using an electric mixer on high speed, beat egg whites until stiff peaks form. Gently but thoroughly fold into pudding mixture. Chill thoroughly.

At time of serving, gently remove chocolate circles from waxed paper and place on 5 individual dessert plates, preferably well-chilled plates.

Spoon equal portions of pudding mixture on top of chocolate puddles and sprinkle cookie crumbs on top. Serve immediately.

SERVES 5; 4.5 FAT GRAMS AND 27% CALORIES FROM FAT PER SERVING.

Hot Apples and Cold "Cream"

Individual frozen yogurt cups topped with hot, rich, spiced apple slices

- 2 cups frozen nonfat vanilla yogurt
- ¾ cup apple juice
- 1½ teaspoons cornstarch
- ½ teaspoon vanilla, butter, and nut flavoring
- ½ teaspoon apple pie spice
- ½ teaspoon granulated sugar
- 1 cup Red Delicious peeled apple slices

Spoon ½ cup frozen yogurt into each of four 6-ounce glass custard cups. Place in freezer until time of serving.

In small saucepan, combine apple juice; cornstarch; vanilla, butter, and nut flavoring; apple pie spice and sugar. Stir well until cornstarch dissolves. Add apples to saucepan. Bring to a boil. Reduce heat and simmer, covered, for 3–4 minutes. Uncover, increase to high heat, and cook 1 minute longer, or until apples are just tender. Remove from heat and let stand uncovered 5 minutes.

At time of serving, spoon equal amounts of hot apples over each serving. Serve immediately.

SERVES 4; 0.2 FAT GRAM AND 0.1% CALORIES FROM FAT PER SERVING.

Variation: Substitute 2 cups ice milk for frozen yogurt. Each serving contains approximately 3 fat grams and 19% calories from fat.

Hot Cherry Sauce over Vanilla Ice Milk

Cherries and their juice, lightly sweetened, heated, thickened, and generously spooned over vanilla ice milk

- 1 16-ounce can sour pitted cherries, undrained
- 3 tablespoons granulated sugar
- 1 tablespoon plus 1½ teaspoons cornstarch
- Few drops red food coloring
- 3 cups vanilla ice milk

In small saucepan, combine cherries, their liquid, sugar, and cornstarch. Mix well until cornstarch dissolves. Bring to a boil and continue boiling 1 minute. Remove from heat, stir in food coloring. Let stand 15 minutes to absorb sweetness.

Place ½ cup ice milk in each of 6 dessert dishes and spoon even amounts of cherry sauce over each.

SERVES 6; 2.9 FAT GRAMS AND 17% CALORIES FROM FAT PER SERVING.

Strawberry-Amaretto Parfait

Layers of frozen yogurt and fresh strawberries, with drizzled liqueur

2 cups quartered strawberries
2 teaspoons granulated sugar
2 cups frozen nonfat vanilla
   yogurt

1 tablespoon plus 1 teaspoon
   amaretto liqueur
4 whole strawberries with stems
   for garnish

In mixing bowl, combine quartered strawberries and sugar. Toss gently but thoroughly and let stand 30 minutes.

At time of serving, in each of 4 parfait dishes or wine goblets, spoon 2 tablespoons frozen yogurt, 2 tablespoons strawberries, repeat frozen yogurt and strawberries. Drizzle each serving with ½ teaspoon amaretto. Spoon 2 tablespoons frozen yogurt, 2 tablespoons strawberries, repeat frozen yogurt, strawberries. Top each with remaining ½ teaspoon amaretto and garnish with whole strawberry. Serve immediately.

SERVES 4; 0.3 FAT GRAM AND 2% CALORIES FROM FAT PER SERVING.

Variation: *Substitute ice milk for frozen yogurt. Each serving contains 3.1 fat grams and 19% calories from fat.*

Sweet Pies, Tarts, and Pastries

Autumn's Deep-Dish Pumpkin Pie

Flavors of the holidays presented in a golden pastry

Butter-flavored low-calorie cooking spray
3 phyllo sheets
2 cups (16 ounces) canned pumpkin
1/3 cup granulated sugar
1/3 cup reduced-calorie maple syrup
1/2 cup egg substitute
1 cup skimmed evaporated milk
1 teaspoon ground cinnamon
1/2 teaspoon ground nutmeg
1/4 teaspoon ground ginger
1/8 teaspoon ground allspice
1/2 teaspoon vanilla, butter, and nut flavoring
1/4 teaspoon salt
1 cup light whipped topping

Preheat oven to 425 degrees.

Coat a 9-inch deep-dish glass pie pan with low-calorie cooking spray. Cut 3 sheets of phyllo in quarters; arrange in pie pan overlapping each other. Spray with cooking spray. Press in center to fit bottom and tuck edges in to give a ruffled appearance.

In mixing bowl, combine pumpkin; sugar; maple syrup; egg substitute; milk; cinnamon; nutmeg; ginger; allspice; vanilla, butter, and nut flavoring; and salt. Mix well and pour into phyllo pie crust. Bake 10 minutes. Reduce heat to 325 degrees and continue baking 45 minutes longer or until knife inserted in center comes out clean. Place on wire rack to cool to room temperature. Place in refrigerator to chill thoroughly.

At time of serving, place 2 tablespoons whipped topping on each serving.

SERVES 8; 1.5 FAT GRAMS AND 9% CALORIES FROM FAT PER SERVING.

THE COUNTY FAIR'S LEMON MERINGUE PIE

Old-fashioned lemon pie served in a beautiful phyllo shell and topped with a golden-tipped meringue

Butter-flavored low-calorie cooking spray
1 phyllo sheet
1 cup granulated sugar, divided
3 tablespoons cornstarch
⅛ teaspoon salt
1 cup water
2 egg yolks, beaten

2 tablespoons diet margarine
2 teaspoons grated lemon rind
3 tablespoons lemon juice
Few drops yellow food coloring
3 egg whites, room temperature
¼ teaspoon cream of tartar
½ teaspoon vanilla extract

Preheat oven to 350 degrees.

Coat a 9-inch pie pan with low-calorie cooking spray. Cut a sheet of phyllo in quarters; place in pie pan overlapping each other. Spray with cooking spray. Press gently to fit bottom of pan and tuck edges under to form a ruffled appearance. Bake 4–6 minutes or until golden.

In medium saucepan, combine ¾ cup plus 2 tablespoons of the sugar, cornstarch, salt, and water. Using a whisk, blend well until cornstarch dissolves. Over medium heat, cook until mixture thickens and comes to a boil, stirring with a flat spatula. Continue boiling 1 minute. Remove from heat. With electric mixer, beat in egg yolks a little at a time. Return to medium heat and cook 3–5 minutes longer until mixture thickens a bit more. Remove from heat, stir in margarine, lemon rind, lemon juice, and food coloring. Pour into baked pie shell and set aside.

In small bowl, with clean beaters, beat egg whites on high speed until soft peaks form. Gradually add remaining 2 tablespoons sugar, cream of tartar, and vanilla extract. Beat until stiff peaks form, being careful not to overbeat.

Spoon on top of filling, making sure edges are sealed. Bake 15 minutes or until tips are browned. Place on wire rack to cool to room temperature, then refrigerate to chill thoroughly, approximately 3 hours.

SERVES 8; 2.9 FAT GRAMS AND 17% CALORIES FROM FAT PER SERVING.

CROWNED COCONUT "CREAM" PIE

Delicious vanilla cream custard made with moist and sweet coconut with a beautiful phyllo crust, crowned with golden-tipped meringue

Butter-flavored low-calorie cooking spray
1 phyllo sheet
6 tablespoons granulated sugar, divided
3 tablespoons plus 1½ teaspoons cornstarch
2 cups skim milk
¼ teaspoon salt

¼ cup egg substitute
1⅓ cups (3½-ounce can) flaked coconut, divided
½ teaspoon Molly McButter
1½ teaspoons vanilla extract, divided
1 teaspoon coconut extract
3 egg whites, room temperature
¼ teaspoon cream of tartar

Preheat oven to 350 degrees.

Coat a 9-inch pie pan with low-calorie cooking spray. Cut sheet of phyllo in quarters; place in pie pan overlapping each other. Spray with cooking spray. Press gently to fit bottom of pan and tuck edges under to give a ruffled appearance. Bake 4–6 minutes until golden.

In medium saucepan, combine ¼ cup of the sugar, cornstarch, milk, and salt. Using whisk, blend well until cornstarch dissolves. Over medium heat, cook until mixture thickens and begins to boil, stirring with a flat spatula. Continue boiling 1 minute. Remove from heat.

In a small bowl, add egg substitute. Pour in 2 tablespoons of the milk mixture, whisk until well blended, and slowly pour egg mixture into milk mixture in medium saucepan, stirring rapidly to avoid lumping. Over medium heat, cook 5 minutes longer, stirring constantly until mixture thickens. Remove from heat. Stir in 1 cup of the coconut, Molly McButter, 1 teaspoon of the vanilla extract, and all of the coconut extract. Stir well and pour into baked pie shell.

In small mixing bowl, using an electric mixer on high speed, beat egg whites to soft peaks. Gradually add remaining 2 tablespoons sugar, cream of tartar, and the remaining ½ teaspoon vanilla extract. Beat until stiff peaks form, being careful not to overbeat. Spoon over filling, making sure edges are sealed with meringue. Sprinkle with the remaining ⅓ cup coconut and bake 15 minutes. Cool on wire rack and then refrigerate 3 hours or until chilled thoroughly.

SERVES 8; 4.1 FAT GRAMS AND 25% CALORIES FROM FAT PER SERVING.

FRESH STRAWBERRY PIE

This is outstanding when berries are in the peak of their season

6 graham crackers
2 tablespoons diet margarine
4 cups quartered ripe strawberries
1¼ cups water
2 tablespoons plus 1½ teaspoons cornstarch

½ cup granulated sugar
Dash of salt
Few drops red food coloring
1 cup light whipped topping

Preheat oven to 400 degrees.

Coat 9-inch pie pan with low-calorie cooking spray. In processor, combine graham crackers and margarine. Blend to coarse meal texture and press into bottom of pie pan. Bake 4 minutes. Cool completely. Place all strawberries in prepared pie pan and set aside.

In small saucepan, combine water, cornstarch, sugar, and salt. Blend until cornstarch has dissolved. Over high heat, bring to a boil and continue boiling 1 minute or until slightly thickened. Cool slightly, add food coloring, if desired, and pour evenly over berries. Chill thoroughly about 3 hours. At time of serving, top each with 1 tablespoon whipped topping.

SERVES 8; 4.3 FAT GRAMS AND 26% CALORIES FROM FAT PER SERVING.

Variation: *Use whole, not quartered, strawberries, if extra sweet, arranging them with points up.*

PINEAPPLE MOUSSE PIE

A mellow whipped blend of sweetened pineapple and creamy vanilla with a hint of orange, mounded in a graham cracker crust

6 graham crackers, crushed
2 tablespoons plus 1½ teaspoons diet margarine, melted
2 packages unflavored gelatin
1 16-ounce can crushed pineapple in heavy syrup, drained, reserving juice

2 egg whites, room temperature
7 tablespoons granulated sugar
⅛ teaspoon salt
2 cups nonfat vanilla yogurt
1 teaspoon grated orange rind
1 teaspoon vanilla extract

Preheat oven to 400 degrees.

Combine graham crackers and margarine in 10-inch pie pan coated with a low-calorie cooking spray. Press crumb mixture evenly over bottom of pan and bake 4 minutes. Cool completely.

In a small saucepan, sprinkle gelatin over reserved pineapple juice; let stand 1 minute. Stir over low heat until gelatin is completely dissolved. Remove from heat to cool.

In medium mixing bowl, using an electric mixer on high speed, beat egg whites to soft peaks, add sugar 1 tablespoon at a time, and whip to stiff peaks.

Combine pineapple, salt, yogurt, orange rind, vanilla extract, and juice and gelatin mixture. Fold in egg whites and spoon into prepared pie crust. Chill at least 3 hours.

SERVES 10; 2.7 FAT GRAMS AND 16% CALORIES FROM FAT PER SERVING.

Summertime Sweet "Cream" Lime Pie

Creamy lime mousse pie crowned with summer's sweet strawberries

6 graham crackers, crushed	1 teaspoon grated lime rind
2 tablespoons diet margarine	3 cups light whipped topping
½ cup limeade concentrate	3 cups halved ripe strawberries
1½ cups light vanilla yogurt	2 tablespoons powdered sugar

Coat a 9-inch springform pan with low-calorie cooking spray. Combine crumbs and margarine in pan. Blend thoroughly and press down evenly over bottom of pan. Bake 4 minutes. Cool completely.

In medium mixing bowl, combine limeade concentrate, yogurt, and grated lime rind. Blend thoroughly. Fold in whipped topping and spoon into prepared pie pan. Chill overnight or at least 3 hours.

Before serving, uniformly arrange strawberries on top, cut side down, and sift powdered sugar over berries. Refrigerate 15 minutes and serve.

SERVES 10; 5 FAT GRAMS AND 30% CALORIES FROM FAT PER SERVING.

CLASSIC TROPICAL FRUIT TART

An array of fresh bananas, kiwis, mangoes, strawberries, and pineapple beautifully arranged on a sweet coconut base and coated with a light pineapple glaze

1⅓ cups (3½-ounce can) loosely packed flaked coconut

⅓ cup all-purpose flour

2 egg whites

1 tablespoon diet margarine, melted

1 teaspoon coconut extract

⅛ teaspoon salt

⅔ cup unsweetened pineapple juice

1 teaspoon cornstarch

2 tablespoons granulated sugar

1 cup sliced bananas

1 kiwi, peeled, thinly sliced, slices halved

1 cup mango, peeled and thinly sliced

1 cup sliced strawberries

½ cup canned crushed pineapple, in its own juice

Preheat oven to 425 degrees.

Coat a 9-inch springform pan with low-calorie cooking spray.

Combine coconut, flour, egg whites, margarine, coconut extract, and salt. Mix thoroughly. Using the back of a fork, spread and press coconut mixture evenly over bottom and up side of pan, about ½ inch.

Bake about 5 minutes or until edges begin to brown. Cool completely.

While crust is baking, in a small saucepan, combine pineapple juice, cornstarch, and sugar. Mix well until cornstarch dissolves. Bring to a boil and continue boiling 1 minute. Let stand 10–15 minutes to cool slightly.

When crust has cooled, arrange fruit decoratively, placing pineapple in center of pie, and spoon sauce evenly over fruit. Chill thoroughly until fruit has set, about 1 hour. Remove side of pan and serve.

SERVES 8; 4.9 FAT GRAMS AND 30% CALORIES FROM FAT PER SERVING.

Fresh Berry Tart with Lemon Crust

A beautiful arrangement of fresh berries on a lightly sweetened lemon crust, glazed to sweeten and enhance completely

¾ cup all-purpose flour
3 tablespoons granulated sugar
2 tablespoons plus 2 teaspoons cold margarine
1 tablespoon grated lemon rind
1 tablespoon lemon juice
1 teaspoon vanilla extract

⅓ cup low-sugar strawberry spread
¼ cup low-sugar raspberry spread
3 tablespoons orange juice
1 cup blackberries
2 cups sliced strawberries
½ cup blueberries

Preheat oven to 425 degrees.

In processor, combine flour, sugar, margarine, lemon rind, lemon juice, and vanilla extract. Process to coarse meal texture in food processor. Shape into 4-inch patty, wrap in plastic wrap, and chill 15 minutes. When chilled, roll dough between 2 sheets of plastic wrap lightly dusted with flour to form a thin, 10-inch circle.

Coat a 9-inch springform pan with low-calorie cooking spray and gently place dough on bottom and up sides of pan, about ½ inch.

Place a sheet of foil over pastry and bake 12–14 minutes or until edges turn light brown. Place pan on wire rack to cool completely.

In small saucepan, add strawberry and raspberry spreads and orange juice. Over low heat, warm thoroughly and stir until completely melted; simmer 1 minute.

Immediately brush 2 tablespoons of glaze over pastry. Arrange fruit decoratively in circles, keeping glaze warm while arranging fruit. Drizzle remaining glaze over fruit. Chill 1 hour. Remove sides of pan after chilling.

SERVES 8; 4 FAT GRAMS AND 24% CALORIES FROM FAT PER SERVING.

Fresh Peach-Apricot Phyllo Tart with Pecans

A golden phyllo tart baked, filled with fresh peaches and peach sauce, seasoned with apricots and maple, topped with toasted pecans

Butter-flavored low-calorie cooking spray
2 phyllo sheets
4 cups sliced fresh or frozen peaches, well drained, divided
2 tablespoons water

½ cup apricot preserves, divided
½ teaspoon grated orange rind
1 tablespoon maple syrup
½ teaspoon vanilla, butter, and nut flavoring
⅓ cup (1½ ounces) pecan pieces

Preheat oven to 350 degrees.

Coat a 9-inch pie pan with low-calorie cooking spray. Cut 2 sheets of phyllo in quarters; place in pie pan, overlapping each other. Liberally coat phyllo layers with cooking spray. Press gently to fit bottom of pan and tuck edges under to form a ruffled appearance. Bake 5–6 minutes or until golden. Place on a wire rack to cool completely.

In processor, place 1¼ cups peach slices and water; puree. Spoon mixture into small saucepan along with the ¼ cup preserves. Bring to a boil, reduce heat to medium-high, and cook uncovered 15–20 minutes, stirring frequently, until thickened. Stir in grated orange rind and set aside to cool to room temperature. When cooled, spoon over bottom of baked phyllo crust and arrange remaining peach slices in an accordion fashion. Heat remaining ¼ cup preserves with maple syrup.

Blend well; remove from heat; stir in vanilla, butter, and nut flavoring and drizzle over slices. Sprinkle with pecan pieces. Chill thoroughly at least 1 hour.

SERVES 8; 3.7 FAT GRAMS AND 22% CALORIES FROM FAT PER SERVING.

Variation: *For more nut flavor, toast pecans under broiler 1 minute before sprinkling on top of peaches.*

GLAZED ALMOND PEAR TART

Phyllo-based tart covered with almond slices, topped with fresh pear slices, and baked with a lightly sweetened apple-almond flavored glaze

Butter flavored low-calorie cooking spray
2 phyllo sheets
2 egg whites
½ cup (2½ ounces) almond slices, divided
3 tablespoons plus 2 teaspoons granulated sugar, divided

1 teaspoon almond extract, divided
3 pears, peeled and sliced
½ cup apple juice
½ teaspoon cornstarch

Preheat oven to 400 degrees.

Coat a nonstick baking sheet with low-calorie cooking spray.

Working quickly, cut phyllo sheets in half crosswise and spray with low-calorie cooking spray. Place on top of each other on baking sheet to make 4 layers of phyllo.

In small bowl, combine egg whites, ⅓ cup almond slices, 3 tablespoons of the sugar, and ½ teaspoon of the almond extract. Mix well and spoon evenly over phyllo.

Place pear slices evenly on top of almond mixture. Bake 30 minutes.

In a small saucepan, combine apple juice, remaining 2 teaspoons sugar, and cornstarch. Mix well until cornstarch dissolves. Bring to a boil and continue boiling until thickened, about 1 minute. Remove from heat and stir in ½ teaspoon almond extract.

Pour evenly over pear slices and top with remaining almond slices.

Bake 10 minutes longer.

SERVES 8; 5.1 FAT GRAMS AND 30% CALORIES FROM FAT PER SERVING.

Homestyle Blueberry-Oat Crumble

Natural, sweet blueberries baked with a flavor-filled oat and cinnamon topping

4 cups fresh blueberries *or* 1⅓
    pounds frozen unsweetened
    blueberries
2 tablespoons lemon juice
2 tablespoons cornstarch
1 tablespoon vanilla extract
½ cup plus 1 tablespoon quick-
    cooking oats

7 tablespoons granulated sugar
¼ cup diet margarine
2 tablespoons all-purpose flour
½ teaspoon ground cinnamon
    Dash of salt

Preheat oven to 350 degrees.

Coat a 9-inch × 9-inch baking pan with low-calorie cooking spray.
Place berries in pan. In small jar, combine lemon juice, cornstarch, and
vanilla extract, and mix well until cornstarch dissolves. Pour over berries
and mix thoroughly.

In processor, combine oats, sugar, margarine, flour, cinnamon, and salt.
Process to coarse crumb texture and sprinkle evenly over berry mixture.

Bake, uncovered, 30 minutes. Remove and heat oven to broil. Place pan
no closer than 5 inches away from heat source and broil 1–2 minutes or
until lightly browned. Let stand 25–30 minutes to absorb flavors and cool
slightly before serving.

SERVES 8; 3.5 FAT GRAMS AND 21% CALORIES FROM FAT PER SERVING.

Individual Cherry Cobblers

Dessert cups filled with cherries and sweet filling, topped with a cobbler-type crust, sprinkled with cinnamon sugar

½ cup all-purpose flour
½ teaspoon baking powder
  Dash of salt
 1 tablespoon shortening
 1 tablespoon plus 1½ teaspoons
   skim milk
 1 16-ounce can sour, pitted
   cherries, undrained
½ cup apple juice concentrate
 3 tablespoons plus 1½ teaspoons
   granulated sugar, divided

 1 tablespoon plus 1 teaspoon
   cornstarch
½ teaspoon ground cinnamon,
   divided
 1 teaspoon Molly McButter
¼ teaspoon almond extract
¼ teaspoon vanilla extract
 4 drops red food coloring

Preheat oven to 375 degrees.

Coat five 6-ounce glass baking cups with low-calorie cooking spray.

Place flour, baking powder, salt, and shortening in food processor. Blend until it becomes a coarse meal texture.

Place in bowl. Using a fork, mix milk into pie dough and stir until just blended and dough forms a ball. Lightly mold dough into 5 small balls. Place back in bowl, cover with plastic wrap, and quick-chill 10 minutes in freezer.

Combine cherries, apple juice concentrate, 3 tablespoons of the sugar, cornstarch, ¼ teaspoon of the cinnamon, Molly McButter, almond extract, vanilla extract, and food coloring. Stir until cornstarch dissolves.

Spoon even amounts into the 5 baking cups.

Remove one dough ball at a time from freezer. Place ball on sheet of plastic wrap lightly dusted with flour. Top with second sheet of floured plastic wrap. Roll into a 4-inch circle and place on top of a filled baking cup. Repeat process until all dough has been rolled.

Combine remaining 1½ teaspoons sugar with ¼ teaspoon cinnamon. Mix thoroughly and sprinkle evenly over all cobbler crusts.

Bake 32–35 minutes. Let stand 12–14 minutes before serving to allow flavors to blend.

SERVES 5; 2.8 FAT GRAMS AND 17% CALORIES FROM FAT PER SERVING.

PEACH-BORDEAUX CRISP

A simple fare of peaches baked in rich seasonings and topped with buttery cookie crumbs

2 1-pound cans sliced peaches in light syrup, undrained, reserving ¼ cup syrup
2 tablespoons light brown sugar
1 teaspoon vanilla, butter, and nut flavoring

½ teaspoon ground nutmeg
2 tablespoons cornstarch
14 Pepperidge Farm Bordeaux Cookies

Preheat oven to 325 degrees.

Coat a 9-inch × 9-inch baking pan with low-calorie cooking spray. In pan, place peaches and the syrup except ¼ cup; brown sugar; vanilla, butter, and nut flavoring; and nutmeg. Mix well. In small jar, combine ¼ cup of the peach syrup with cornstarch; shake until cornstarch dissolves completely and add to peach mixture. Blend well. Bake 30 minutes.

Place cookies in processor to make coarse crumb texture.

Remove peaches from oven, and increase heat to broil. Sprinkle peaches with cookie crumbs and place pan no closer than 5 inches away from heat source. Broil 1–2 minutes or until lightly browned. Let stand 10–15 minutes to absorb flavors. Serve warm or room temperature.

SERVES 8; 2.7 FAT GRAMS AND 16% CALORIES FROM FAT PER SERVING.

ALMOND APRICOT-GLAZED "CREAM" PUFFS

Cream puffs filled with frozen yogurt, glazed with apricots, and topped with toasted almonds

½ cup water
2 tablespoons diet margarine
7 tablespoons all-purpose flour
⅛ teaspoon salt
4 egg whites
¾ cup thinly sliced peaches
1 package Equal sweetener

½ cup frozen nonfat vanilla yogurt
1 tablespoon apricot preserves, melted
2 tablespoons (½ ounce) almond slices, toasted and crumbled

Preheat oven to 400 degrees.

In a small saucepan, bring water to a boil. Melt margarine in water. Using a fork, stir in flour and salt. Stir vigorously. Cook and stir until mixture forms a ball. Remove from heat; let stand 10 minutes. With an electric mixer on low speed, beat egg whites into the dough. Beat 1 minute. Batter will be lumpy and a bit runny.

Coat a nonstick cookie sheet with low-calorie cooking spray. Spoon 4 mounds of batter on cookie sheet 3 inches apart. Bake 25–30 minutes or until golden. Remove from oven. Let cool 10 minutes.

While cooling, in a small bowl, combine peaches and Equal. Toss well and set aside 15 minutes.

Using a serrated knife, cut puffs in half horizontally. Spoon 2 tablespoons frozen yogurt in each bottom half of cream puffs. Drain peach slices well and spoon 3 tablespoons over each serving.

Brush heated apricot preserves over tops of cream puffs. Sprinkle almonds on top of apricot glaze and place on top of peaches. Serve immediately or wrap in plastic wrap and freeze until time of serving.

SERVES 4; 4.6 FAT GRAMS AND 27% CALORIES FROM FAT PER SERVING.

CHERRY TURNOVERS WITH CINNAMON SUGAR

Phyllo turnovers overflowing with hot cherry filling and sprinkled with cinnamon sugar

Butter-flavored low-calorie cooking spray

1 16-ounce can sour pitted cherries, undrained

2 tablespoons cornstarch

¼ cup frozen apple juice concentrate

2 tablespoons granulated sugar, divided

1 teaspoon almond extract

6 phyllo sheets

¾ teaspoon ground cinnamon

Preheat oven to 400 degrees.

Coat a nonstick cookie sheet with low-calorie cooking spray.

In small saucepan, combine cherries, cornstarch, apple juice concentrate, and 1 tablespoon plus 1½ teaspoons of the sugar. Blend well until cornstarch is dissolved. Bring to a boil and continue boiling, stirring, 1 minute. Remove from heat and stir in almond extract. Let stand 10 minutes.

Work with 1 phyllo sheet at a time, keeping others covered with a slightly damp cloth.

Coat sheet with low-calorie cooking spray. Fold in half crosswise and coat again. Spoon one-sixth of the cherry mixture, about ⅓ cup, near one end. Fold edges inward and carefully roll up, making about a 3-inch × 4-inch turnover. Place on prepared sheet and repeat process.

Combine the remaining 1½ teaspoons sugar with the cinnamon. Blend well. Coat turnovers with cooking spray and sprinkle evenly with cinnamon sugar mixture. Bake 20 minutes. Remove from oven and let stand 15 minutes before serving.

Serve warm or room temperature.

SERVES 6; 0.6 FAT GRAM AND 3% CALORIES FROM FAT PER SERVING.

CINNAMON SUGARED APPLE TURNOVERS

Phyllo pastry filled and rolled with succulent apples and raisins, sprinkled with cinnamon sugar

Butter-flavored low-calorie cooking spray

2 cups Golden Delicious peeled apple slices

1 cup Granny Smith peeled apple slices

¾ cup apple juice

3 tablespoons raisins, halved

1 tablespoon plus 2 teaspoons cornstarch

1 tablespoon plus 2 teaspoons granulated sugar, divided

1½ teaspoons apple pie spice

⅛ teaspoon salt

½ teaspoon vanilla, butter, and nut flavoring

8 phyllo sheets

¼ teaspoon ground cinnamon

Preheat oven to 400 degrees.

Coat a nonstick cookie sheet with a low-calorie cooking spray.

In a medium saucepan, combine apple slices, apple juice, raisins, cornstarch, 1 tablespoon plus 1 teaspoon of the sugar, apple pie spice, and salt. Mix thoroughly until cornstarch is well blended. Bring to a boil, reduce heat, cover tightly, and simmer 4 minutes. Remove from heat, stir in vanilla, butter, and nut flavoring and let stand covered 15 minutes for easier handling.

Work with 1 phyllo sheet at a time, keeping others covered with a slightly damp cloth.

Coat sheet with low-calorie cooking spray. Fold in half crosswise and coat again. Spoon one-eighth of the apple mixture near one end. Fold edges inward and carefully roll up, making about a 3-inch × 4-inch turnover. Repeat process until done.

Combine the remaining 1 teaspoon sugar with the cinnamon. Blend well. Coat turnovers with cooking spray and sprinkle cinnamon sugar evenly over all. Bake 18 minutes.

Serve warm or room temperature.

SERVES 8; 0.6 FAT GRAM AND 4% CALORIES FROM FAT PER SERVING.

Freshly Baked Cinnamon Rolls

Enjoy these treasures straight from the oven and freshly iced for their greatest rewards

¼ cup apple juice
⅓ cup raisins
2⅓ cups reduced fat buttermilk baking mix
⅔ cup water
1 tablespoon plus 2 teaspoons granulated sugar

1½ teaspoons cinnamon
1 teaspoon vanilla extract
7 tablespoons powdered sugar
2½ teaspoons skim milk

Preheat oven to 450 degrees.

In a small saucepan, combine juice and raisins and bring to a boil. Cover and remove from heat. Let stand 2–3 minutes.

Place raisins and any remaining juice in mixing bowl along with buttermilk baking mix, water, granulated sugar, cinnamon, and vanilla extract. Mix thoroughly.

Coat a nonstick baking sheet with low-calorie cooking spray. Spoon batter in 10 separate mounds and bake 7 minutes, no longer.

While rolls are baking, combine powdered sugar and milk. Mix well and set aside.

When rolls are done, immediately place on a decorative platter and drizzle icing over all.

Serve immediately.

SERVES 10; 1.9 FAT GRAMS AND 12% CALORIES FROM FAT PER SERVING.

FROZEN CHOCOLATE ECLAIRS

Cream puffs filled with frozen yogurt and topped with chocolate sauce

½ cup water
1 tablespoon margarine
⅛ teaspoon salt
7 tablespoons all-purpose flour
½ cup egg substitute
¼ cup semisweet chocolate chips

1¼ teaspoons shortening
2 tablespoons skim milk
1 teaspoon vanilla extract
2⅔ cups frozen nonfat vanilla yogurt

Preheat oven to 400 degrees.

Coat a nonstick cookie sheet with low-calorie cooking spray. In a small saucepan, bring water and margarine to a boil. All at once, add salt and flour, stirring rapidly with fork until it forms a ball. With an electric mixer, slowly beat egg substitute into the dough. Beat 1 minute. Batter will be lumpy and a bit runny. On prepared cookie sheet, spoon and shape 8 mounds each into 1½-inch × 4-inch form, 2 inches apart. Bake 25 minutes.

While eclairs are baking, in small saucepan over low heat, melt chocolate chips and shortening. Stir with a rubber spatula until smooth. Stir in milk and blend until smooth. Remove from heat, add vanilla extract, and refrigerate to chill thoroughly.

When eclairs are done, remove from cookie sheet and cool completely on wire rack. Gently cut in half lengthwise with serrated knife. Spoon ⅓ cup frozen yogurt on bottom half of eclair, top with other half, and spoon 1 teaspoon chilled sauce over top of each eclair; spread evenly with back of spoon. Serve immediately or loosely wrap with plastic wrap and freeze until time of serving.

SERVES 8; 3.4 FAT GRAMS AND 21% CALORIES FROM FAT PER SERVING.

Frozen Kahlua Meringue

A large, crunchy, vanilla meringue topped with frozen yogurt and drizzled with a rich coffee liqueur

2 egg whites, room temperature
¼ teaspoon cream of tartar
Dash of salt
1½ teaspoons vanilla extract

3 tablespoons granulated sugar
1 cup frozen nonfat vanilla *or* chocolate yogurt
¼ cup coffee *or* hazelnut liqueur

Preheat oven to 275 degrees.

Line a cookie sheet with foil.

In a small nonplastic bowl, using an electric mixer on high speed, beat egg whites until foamy. Beat in cream of tartar, salt, and vanilla extract until soft peaks form. Gradually, 1 tablespoon at a time, beat in sugar until stiff peaks form.

Mound meringue in center of cookie sheet. Using back of spoon, shape meringue into one 8-inch circle. Bake 1 hour. Turn off oven. Do not open oven door. Leave meringue in oven 2 hours longer. Remove meringue from oven and place cookie sheet on wire rack to finish cooling for 10 minutes. Gently remove foil and prepare to serve or wrap tightly in plastic wrap until time of serving.

At time of serving, place meringue on decorative platter. Using a tablespoon, spoon frozen yogurt on top of meringue. Drizzle liqueur over all and serve immediately.

SERVES 4; 0 FAT GRAMS AND 0% CALORIES FROM FAT.

Variation: *Substitute ice milk for frozen yogurt. Each serving contains 1.4 fat grams and 8% calories from fat.*

Those Succulent Fruits

Ambrosia's Simplicity

A simple, sweet combination of fresh oranges and coconut

13 medium navel oranges, sectioned

⅔ cup (half a 3½-ounce can) canned flaked coconut

1 tablespoon granulated sugar

In a decorative bowl, combine all ingredients. Cover and refrigerate at least 1 hour.

SERVES 8; 2.9 FAT GRAMS AND 17% CALORIES FROM FAT PER SERVING.

CHILLED HONEYDEW, FRESH PEACHES, AND SWEET CHERRIES IN BLACKBERRY SAUCE

Plates of fresh fruits resting in puddles of lightly sweetened blackberry sauce

1 16-ounce can blackberries in heavy syrup

1 tablespoon granulated sugar

1 teaspoon cornstarch

6 cups melon balls *or* cubes

3 cups peach slices

1½ cups sweet dark cherries, halved and pitted

Place berries and syrup in processor and puree. Drain through cheesecloth-lined colander to remove seeds, using a rubber spatula to press down gently. Place strained berry sauce in small saucepan; add sugar and cornstarch. Stir until cornstarch dissolves. Bring to a boil; continue boiling 1 minute. Place in refrigerator to chill thoroughly.

In large bowl, combine melon balls, peach slices, and cherries. Toss gently and refrigerate until time of serving. At time of serving, spoon 1¾ cups of fruit mixture on individual dessert plates. Stir sauce well and spoon equal portions of sauce (about ¼ cup each) around outer edges of fruit to form a puddle.

SERVES 6; 0.7 FAT GRAM AND 4% CALORIES FROM FAT PER SERVING.

Fresh Bananas in New Orleans "Cream"

Sliced bananas smothered in a sweet vanilla custard sauce

1 cup skim milk	2 teaspoons cornstarch
3 tablespoons granulated sugar	⅛ teaspoon salt
1 tablespoon vanilla extract	3 cups banana slices

In medium saucepan, combine milk, sugar, vanilla extract, cornstarch, and salt. Whisk until cornstarch dissolves.

Over medium-high heat, cook, stirring with a flat spatula, until mixture comes to a boil. Continue boiling 1 minute. Chill thoroughly before serving.

At time of serving, place ¾ cups bananas in each of 4 dessert bowls. Spoon ¼ cup sauce over each serving.

SERVES 4; 0.6 FAT GRAM AND 3% CALORIES FROM FAT PER SERVING.

Fresh Fruit Cassis

Blueberries combined with a delicate liqueur and sparkling club soda

3 cups fresh blueberries
1 cup club soda
¼ cup plus 2 tablespoons crème de cassis

1 tablespoon fresh lime juice
Fresh lime wedges for garnish

In medium mixing bowl, combine berries, club soda, crème de cassis, and lime juice. Toss carefully but quickly. Spoon even amounts in 4 chilled wine goblets; garnish with lime wedges. Be sure to serve immediately to prevent club soda from becoming flat.

SERVES 4; 0.5 FAT GRAM AND 3% CALORIES FROM FAT PER SERVING.

FRUITS FOR A MIDSUMMER'S NIGHT

Fresh melons, sweet cherries, and more tossed with a hint of citrus and served very cold

2 cups cantaloupe cubes
2 cups honeydew cubes
1½ cups dark sweet cherries, halved and pitted
2 cups watermelon cubes

2 tablespoons orange juice concentrate
1 tablespoon plus 2 teaspoons light brown sugar, packed
1 tablespoon grated orange rind

Place all ingredients in decorative bowl. Toss gently but thoroughly. Chill at least 1 hour.

SERVES 4; 1.3 FAT GRAMS AND 8% CALORIES FROM FAT PER SERVING.

The Grandstand

A colorful array of fresh fruits strategically arranged and marinated in a sweet orange liqueur

2 cups cubed honeydew
1 cup halved strawberries
1 cup blueberries
1 medium navel orange, sectioned
2 cups ripe nectarines, sliced

2 kiwis, peeled and thinly sliced
1 cup dark sweet cherries, halved and pitted
⅔ cup orange liqueur
1 teaspoon grated orange rind

In large glass bowl, layer fruit by placing honeydew on bottom of bowl, followed by strawberries, blueberries, orange sections, nectarines, kiwis, and top with cherries.

In separate bowl, combine liqueur and orange rind and mix well. Pour over fruit, cover, and refrigerate 8 hours.

SERVES 8; 0.6 FAT GRAM AND 0% CALORIES FROM FAT PER SERVING.

Mexican Fruits and Crisps

Plates filled with fresh, sweet oranges, mangoes, bananas, and pineapple and served with hot cinnamon-sugar crisps

2 medium navel oranges, sectioned
1 cup banana slices
1 cup canned pineapple chunks in its own juice, drained
1½ cups mango slices

Butter-flavored low-calorie cooking spray
2 10-inch flour tortillas
1 tablespoon margarine, melted
2 tablespoons granulated sugar
Ground cinnamon

Preheat oven to 475 degrees.

In decorative bowl, combine orange sections, bananas, pineapple, and mango slices. Toss gently but thoroughly. Keep refrigerated until serving.

Coat a nonstick cookie sheet with low-calorie cooking spray. Place tortillas on sheet and coat tortillas liberally with spray.

Drizzle melted margarine over tortillas. Using back of spoon, spread margarine to coat evenly. Sprinkle sugar over all. Sprinkle liberally with cinnamon and carefully slice each tortilla in 6 even wedges. Bake on cookie sheet 3 minutes.

Spoon equal amounts of fruit onto 6 dessert plates and place 2 wedges on each.

Serve immediately while crisps are warm.

SERVES 6; 3 FAT GRAMS AND 19% CALORIES FROM FAT PER SERVING.

SANGRIA FRUITS

Fresh, sweet oranges and red grapes marinated in a spiced red wine, served in frozen wine goblets

1 cup dry red wine
½ cup water
3 tablespoons sugar
½ stick cinnamon
4 whole cloves

2 slices lemon
8 medium navel oranges, sectioned
1½ cups (approximately 50) seedless red grapes, halved

In small saucepan, combine wine, water, sugar, cinnamon, cloves, and lemon slices. Mix well. Bring to a boil and continue boiling 2 minutes. Remove from heat. Cool.

Place oranges and grapes in medium mixing bowl. Toss gently. Pour cooled wine mixture over fruit. Toss again and chill thoroughly.

Serve in frozen wine goblets.

SERVES 6; 0.2 FAT GRAM AND 1% CALORIES FROM FAT PER SERVING.

Skewered Fruit with Sweet "Cream" Fondue

Fresh summer fruits pierced with toothpicks and dipped in a honey-sweetened yogurt with a hint of orange

1½ cups nonfat plain yogurt
2 tablespoons honey
1 teaspoon grated orange rind
1 teaspoon vanilla extract

2 cups fresh peaches cut in 1-inch pieces
2 cups quartered strawberries
1 cup seedless green grapes

In small bowl, combine yogurt, honey, orange rind, and vanilla extract. Mix well and spoon equal portions into 4 individual sauce cups or 1 small decorative bowl. Place fruit in separate bowl and toss gently.

Serve on 4 individual dessert plates or 1 decorative platter along with honeyed yogurt. Serve with toothpicks.

SERVES 4; 0.4 FAT GRAM AND 2% CALORIES FROM FAT PER SERVING.

BAKED APPLES AND PECANS

Apple slices baked with a mild maple flavor and topped with buttery-flavored pecans

2 cups Red Delicious apple slices
1 cup Granny Smith apple slices
¼ cup plus 2 tablespoons pecan pieces

¼ cup maple syrup
2 teaspoons Molly McButter
½ teaspoon vanilla, butter, and nut flavoring

Preheat oven to 350 degrees.

Coat a 9-inch × 9-inch square baking pan with low-calorie cooking spray. Place Red Delicious and Granny Smith apple slices in pan and toss until well blended. Thoroughly combine pecans; syrup; Molly McButter; and vanilla, butter, and nut flavoring. Spoon evenly on apples and bake 25 minutes or until tender-crisp. Remove from oven. Serve immediately.

SERVES 6; 5 FAT GRAMS AND 30% CALORIES FROM FAT PER SERVING.

BAKED APPLES OF SEPTEMBER

Succulent apples slowly baked, filled with pecans, raisins, and spices

3 tablespoons pecan chips
1 tablespoon plus 1 teaspoon granulated sugar
1 tablespoon plus 1 teaspoon raisins, halved
1 tablespoon plus 1 teaspoon water
2 teaspoons diet margarine

1 teaspoon vanilla, butter, and nut flavoring
1 teaspoon ground cinnamon
½ teaspoon ground nutmeg
4 medium Red Delicious *or* Jonathan apples, halved and cored

Preheat oven to 325 degrees.

In small saucepan, combine pecans; sugar; raisins; water; margarine; vanilla, butter, and nut flavoring; cinnamon; and nutmeg; heat until margarine has melted. Stir well.

Coat a 9-inch × 13-inch baking pan with low-calorie cooking spray. Place halved apples in pan and spoon approximately 2 teaspoons of the filling in each apple half. Bake, uncovered, 45–50 minutes or until apples are tender.

SERVES 4; 4.9 FAT GRAMS AND 29% CALORIES FROM FAT PER SERVING.

Baked Caribbean Bananas

Bananas baked in a warm blend of spices and topped with frozen yogurt

⅓ cup unsweetened pineapple
  juice
1 tablespoon plus 2 teaspoons
  dark brown sugar, packed
½ teaspoon vanilla, butter, and
  nut flavoring

¼ teaspoon ground cinnamon
⅛ teaspoon ground nutmeg
2½ cups sliced ripe bananas
1 cup frozen nonfat vanilla
  yogurt

Preheat oven to 350 degrees.

In mixing bowl, combine juice; sugar; vanilla, butter, and nut flavoring; cinnamon; and nutmeg. Mix thoroughly. Add bananas. Toss gently but thoroughly to coat.

Coat a nonstick 8-inch baking pan or four 6-ounce glass baking cups with low-calorie cooking spray. Spoon banana mixture into pan or cups and bake 20 minutes uncovered. Let stand 10–15 minutes to absorb flavors.

Serve warm, topped with ¼ cup frozen yogurt per serving.

SERVES 4; 0.4 FAT GRAM AND 2% CALORIES FROM FAT PER SERVING.

Variation: *Substitute 1 cup ice milk for frozen nonfat yogurt. Each serving contains 1.8 fat grams and 11% calories from fat.*

FATHER JIM'S CHUNKY APPLESAUCE

Down-home flavors and childhood memories

6 cups Red Delicious peeled apple
  slices
2 tablespoons dark brown sugar,
  packed

1 teaspoon ground cinnamon
¼ cup light whipped topping,
  optional

In 2-quart saucepan, combine all ingredients except whipped topping. Toss thoroughly and cover tightly. Over medium-low heat, cook 15–20 minutes. Stir and mash with fork, if necessary, to blend well. Remove from heat; let stand, covered, 10 minutes. Serve warm or chill thoroughly. Serve each with 1 tablespoon of whipped topping, if desired.

SERVES 4; 0.8 FAT GRAM AND 5% CALORIES FROM FAT PER SERVING WITHOUT WHIPPED TOPPING, *OR* 1.3 FAT GRAMS AND 8% CALORIES FROM FAT PER SERVING WITH WHIPPED TOPPING.

Sweet, Hot, and Spiced Pineapple Skewers

Broiled quick and close to the flame to capture the sweet juices

4 12-inch bamboo skewers	Whole cloves
3 cups drained pineapple chunks, packed in its own juice	¼ cup dark brown sugar, packed
	1 teaspoon Molly McButter

Preheat oven to broil.

Line broiler pan with a sheet of foil.

Thread ¾ cup pineapple chunks on each skewer. Place a whole clove in each chunk. Combine brown sugar and Molly McButter. Mix thoroughly. Place skewered pineapple on broiler pan; carefully sprinkle brown sugar mixture on top of pineapple.

Broil 2–3 inches from heat source, about 6 minutes.

Place on individual dessert plates, drizzle any remaining juices over all. Remove cloves. Serve immediately.

SERVES 4; 0.2 FAT GRAM AND 1% CALORIES FROM FAT PER SERVING.

SWEETENED GRAPEFRUIT

Quick-broiled with dark sugar and left standing to absorb its sweet syrup

4 whole grapefruits, halved
⅓ cup plus 1 tablespoon plus 1
    teaspoon dark brown sugar,
    packed

Preheat oven to broil.

Cut and loosen each section in grapefruit halves, leaving them in place.

Mound 2½ teaspoons brown sugar on top of each grapefruit half. Place on foil-lined baking sheet and broil no closer than 5 inches from heat source 6–7 minutes. Remove from oven. Let stand 10 minutes before serving. Place 2 halves on each dessert plate, drizzle any remaining juices over all.

SERVES 4; 0.2 FAT GRAM AND 1% CALORIES FROM FAT PER SERVING.

VANILLA POACHED PEARS

Fresh pears simmered and chilled in a sweet and delicate syrup

1 cup semisweet white wine
⅔ cup water
¼ cup plus 1 tablespoon sugar
¼ cup honey

6 fresh pears, unpeeled, halved,
  cored, and cut in ½-inch slices
2 tablespoons vanilla extract

In medium saucepan, combine wine, water, sugar, and honey. Bring to a boil and continue boiling 2 minutes. Add pears. Toss to coat. Return to a boil, reduce heat, cover tightly, and simmer 4 minutes or until just tender.

Remove from heat, add vanilla extract, and stir well. Place pears and syrup in a nonmetal container, cool uncovered to room temperature, then cover and chill thoroughly, about 3 hours. Stir occasionally to prevent discoloring and to absorb flavors evenly.

SERVES 6; 0.7 FAT GRAM AND 4% CALORIES FROM FAT PER SERVING.

Big Pig,
Little Pig

By Marcia Vaughan
Illustrated by Lois Ehlert

ScottForesman

A Division of HarperCollinsPublishers

Big pig, big pig, turn around.

Little pig, little pig, roll on the ground.

Big sheep, big sheep, sleep in the sun.

4

Little sheep, little sheep, leap and run.

5

Big horse, big horse, pull the plow.

6

Little horse, little horse, chase the cow.

Animals, animals,
move your feet.
Animals, animals,
it's time to eat!